D0891499

THEOCRACY AND ESCHATOLOGY

THEOCRACY
AND
ESCHATOLOGY

by

OTTO PLÖGER
Professor of Old Testament Studies,
University of Heidelberg

translated by

S. RUDMAN
Lecturer in Religious Education,
West Midlands College of Education

JOHN KNOX PRESS
RICHMOND · VIRGINIA

Translated from the second German edition
by permission of
NEUKIRCHENER VERLAG

American edition published by
John Knox Press, Richmond, Virginia

Library of Congress Catalog Card Number: 68–12142

Printed in Great Britain

CONTENTS

PREFACE TO THE ENGLISH EDITION

THE English translation is based on the second edition which appeared in 1962; apart from minor corrections there were no alterations to the first edition of 1959. It seemed best to adopt the same text for this translation in order to present the hypothesis in its original form. Apart from certain reservations which I have had from the beginning, the fact that I would phrase some of the sections differently is due not least to the various criticisms, for which I am most grateful. Such a revision, however, would not affect the total conception of the work so much as the textual analysis; in fact, my detailed study of the Book of Daniel (cf. my commentary which is about to be published, KAT XVIII) had already suggested this. I should wish to bring into the discussion some chapters from Trito-Isaiah either instead of or in addition to the analysis of the Book of Joel, in that these chapters seek an eschatological solution to the acute contemporary problem of a cleavage between those who rebelled against Yahweh (*Jahweverächter*) and those who worshipped Yahweh (cf. especially Isa. lxv). My hope of contributing to the understanding of the Isaiah–Apocalypse (Isa. xxiv–xxvii) has not been fulfilled, however. Thus, the hope expressed on the final page holds good for the English edition also; it is also worth repeating because English and American scholarship have for many years given special attention to the latest period of the Old Testament.

I am greatly indebted to the English and German publishers, to the former for undertaking the translation and to the latter for suggesting and encouraging the English edition.

Bonn, April 1964. OTTO PLÖGER

FOREWORD

THE aim of the present study, the title of which could have been taken from a compendium of dogmatics, is not to discuss a problem of systematic theology. Its aim is far more modest: namely, to investigate a historical problem and suggest a possible fresh solution.

The monarchical period of Israel brings with it a large number of prophetic figures. The more the two kingdoms, Ephraim and Judah, threaten to fall prey to ancient Oriental powers, the more the prophets proclaim the universal dominion of their God. With the loss of national sovereignty—after a short revival, in which the restoration of the destroyed temple at Jerusalem was undertaken—the successors of the prophetic movement retreated into anonymity, and only later additions and supplements to the writings of their great predecessors inform us of their existence. Israel itself regarded this late period of its history as a period without prophets, and we may well echo the lament of the Psalmist (Ps. lxxiv. 9), if we look back to the envoys of the prophetic spirit and ask where they have disappeared to.

About three hundred years later the Jewish community, the successor of ancient Israel and now part of a Hellenistic kingdom, is involved in a serous clash with the power of the state, in the course of which an armed insurrection breaks out and the rebuilding of a Jewish kingdom is undertaken. But the men who take part in this insurrection obviously come from different camps. Beside the forces which—after the surprising initial successes—are quite ready to risk the fight for power, stands a comparatively unknown group, the 'Pious', who are praised for their loyalty to the Law and their courageous faith. We are anxious to discover if it is accurate to regard the Book of Daniel, which was one of the last books to be received into the Canon of the Old Testament, as evidence of the spirit of these 'Pious'. We are justified, therefore, in asking where the 'Pious', the *Hasidim*, come from.

These two questions define, at least approximately, the period which is to be scrutinized in this essay from one particular point of view.

ABBREVIATIONS

ANVAO	*Avhandlinger utgitt av Det Norske Videnskaps-Akademi i Oslo*
ATD	Das Alte Testament Deutsch
BH	*Biblia Hebraica* (ed. R. Kittel)
BWANT	Beiträge zur Wissenschaft vom Alten und Neuen Testament
BZAW	Beihefte zur *Zeitschrift für die alttestamentliche Wissenschaft*
EB	Etudes Bibliques
HAT	Handbuch zum Alten Testament
HK	Handkommentar zum Alten Testament
HSAT	*Die Heilige Schrift des Alten Testaments*
HUCA	*Hebrew Union College Annual*
ICC	International Critical Commentary
KAT	Kommentar zum Alten Testament
KHC	Kurzer Hand-Commentar zum Alten Testament
RB	*Revue Biblique*
ThR	*Theologische Rundschau*
ThWB	*Theologisches Wörterbuch zum Neuen Testament*
TSK	*Theologische Studien und Kritiken*
VT	*Vetus Testamentum*
ZAW	*Zeitschrift für die alttestamentliche Wissenschaft*
ZDPV	*Zeitschrift des deutschen Palästina Vereins*
ZThK	*Zeitschrift für Theologie und Kirche*

CHAPTER I

HISTORICAL INTRODUCTION

'RELIGIOUS conflict' is certainly an accurate description of Antiochus IV Epiphanes' dealings with the Jewish community in Jerusalem, in so far as there were definite attacks by the king on the cultic integrity of the Jerusalem community; if it is intended as a description of the Seleucid overlord's policy in principle, however, it needs to be qualified slightly. Otherwise it would be an encroachment of outstanding importance to which neither Persian nor Ptolemaic rule offered a parallel; even under Antiochus III, the father of Epiphanes, no such step can be demonstrated, for the privileged position of the Jewish community was expressly confirmed when Palestine passed into the sphere of Seleucid rule. The unparalleled attack of the Syrian king constantly raises the question, what special purposes may be descried behind the new policy of Antiochus.[1] Even in antiquity historians gave different explanations; over against the rationalistic explanation (of Polybius), which refers to the chronic financial difficulties of the Seleucids and attributes special significance to the plundering of the Temple in Jerusalem, the more ideologically coloured explanation (of Diodorus and Tacitus), according to which Antiochus acted as the champion of Hellenistic civilization against Jewish barbarism, has won wider approval.[2] There is no doubt that general political considerations played a part in all this, for the establishment of their kingdom, which had been weakened by Roman pressure, must have been of special concern to the Seleucids.[3] Bickermann has gone into these questions more fully in his instructive

[1] E. Bickermann, *Der Gott der Makkabäer* (1937); cf. also his survey, *Die Makkabäer* (1935). H. L. Jansen, *Die Politik Antiochos des IV* (1943). F. M. Abel, *Histoire de la Palestine* I (1952), pp. 109f. M. Noth, *History of Israel* (1960[2]), pp. 359ff.

[2] Difficulties, however, are created by the fact that there is not always a clear distinction between rulers of the same name, so that sometimes Antiochus VII Sidetes may be referred to.

[3] Jansen comes to this conclusion in his book referred to above; cf. p. 39: 'Everything points to the fact that A. (Antiochus IV) regarded his political mission as a strengthening of internal ties. The dissolution movement had assumed such proportions that the idea of unity within the borders had to be realised partly through the extermination of rebellious elements, partly through the elimination of the reason for the rebellion'—Jansen is thinking here of the temple-confiscations— 'and through the construction of symbols that would unite people.'

I

study referred to above. His work, written, it is significant, at the time of the pre-war conflict within the church in Germany ('Kirchen-kampf'), directs our attention expressly to internal Jewish relation-ships. Thus, he takes up the 'prophetic' explanation of events given in the Bible, for example, in the Book of Daniel, according to which Israel's disobedience has called forth God's punishment. Bickermann, however, was not altogether able to avoid drawing a too neutral, and at times too favourable, picture of Antiochus. Various motives may have determined the way the king acted, imponderables which are often at work when a change of ruler takes place, but which were especially so in the case of Antiochus, because after his ten year absence in Rome as a hostage he undoubtedly had a one-sided view of relationships in the East and was, furthermore, not originally expected to be the ruler. Nor should the religious, ideological colour-ing of kingship, bequeathed by Oriental divine kingship, be under-estimated, however offensive it may have been to Jewish ears that it should have been taken up in the titulature of liberal-minded Hellenistic rulers, who described themselves as *Theos* ('God') or *Epiphanes* (*Theos*). Yet it is still an open question whether the immediate reason for the unusual way in which Antiochus acted should not be sought in the special political situation in Palestine at that time.

When Antiochus IV (175 B.C.) assumed power, Palestine, and hence the territory of the Jewish community, had been in the possession of the Seleucids for only twenty years. We can hardly assume that the new régime was already firmly established after such a comparatively short period; it would have required a fairly long period of peace, but, in fact, the opposite had been the case. Antiochus III, the father of Antiochus Epiphanes, had contemplated the conquest of Syria and Palestine ever since his coronation, but after his defeat at Raphia (217 B.C.) no further attempt was made, at least while Ptolemy IV Philopator was alive, and he devoted his attention to the East of his kingdom. Immediately after the death of Philopator, however, he made a secret agreement with Philip of Macedonia to divide up the Ptolemaic possessions in Asia; but he was so annoyed at Philip's persistent advances into Asia Minor that on the outbreak of the Macedonian War he was persuaded by a Roman embassy to adopt a position of neutrality, which gave him a free hand in Asia Minor and also in southern Syria and Palestine. In the course of that year he penetrated as far as Gaza with the support of the Jews—he refers to this in the decrees quoted in

Josephus (Ant. xii. 3.3)[4]—but, being tied in Asia Minor, he was not able to maintain the success of his victorious march in the face of the able Ptolemaic general Scopas; it was not until his victory at Paneion (near the source of the Jordan) that the fate of Palestine was decided (198 B.C.). After the defeat of Macedonia Rome could not quietly accept this growth of power in the southern part of the Seleucid kingdom, increased by the gain of the Ptolemaic areas of Asia Minor, which Philip had originally possessed. Hence the negotiations; but Antiochus acted shrewdly in making known his indifference to Greece in return for a free hand in Asia Minor. Did he have far-reaching plans? His hasty march to Egypt when he received news of the young Ptolemy V Epiphanes' death—this turned out to be mistaken, however, whereupon Antiochus immediately broke off his undertaking—suggests that he was considering the possibility of occupying Egypt and must, therefore, have had considerable interest in occupying Palestine. Contrary to what might reasonably have been expected, however, the Romans did not intervene in favour of the Ptolemies in the matter of the occupation of southern Syria and Palestine; if it was contemplated, Antiochus knew how to thwart Roman plans, for in 194 B.C. he married his daughter Cleopatra to the Egyptian king. When Josephus (Ant. xii. 4.1) speaks of Antiochus having promised Coile-Syria, Samaria, Judaea and Phoenicia as a dowry, then this can only mean—if the report in its present form is accurate—that Antiochus was acting dynastically and hoping for the patronage of the Ptolemies by degrees and was in this sense giving the Egyptian court a share in the revenue of the former Ptolemaic regions.[5] At any rate, the Seleucids successfully attempted to maintain freedom of action in Asia without becoming involved in conflict with Rome. That this could not be avoided much longer must have been clear to Antiochus; it was not accidental that he offered hospitality at his court to the fugitive Hannibal at that time. Sooner than he desired, however, the unsettled state of Greece, which was torn by opposing factions following the defeat of Macedonia, drew him into war with Rome; the details of this are not important for our present study, but it ended after several years in the peace of Apamaea (189–188 B.C.) with the overthrow of the empire Antiochus had striven to build. Surprisingly, in a treaty which almost completely excluded the Seleucids from Asia

---

[4] On the decrees of Antiochus III quoted in Josephus cf. A. Alt, *ZAW* (1939), pp. 283f.
[5] Cf. A. Bouché-Leclerq, *Histoire des Séleucides* (1913), pp. 572f.

Minor, the Syro-Palestinian question was not even mentioned. Was Rome annoyed at the marriage of its Egyptian ally with a Seleucid princess, or was it aiming to avoid a further weakening of the Seleucid kingdom following its defeat, lest this should give the Ptolemies the upper hand in Asia and encourage further expansion into the former Ptolemaic territories in Asia Minor? In short, Antiochus retained possession of the regions taken from the Ptolemies and thereby his superiority over Egypt, which was protected by its possession of southern Syria and Palestine. The disappointment of Egypt and its Seleucid princess on the throne in Alexandria was understandable, especially since the position of the crown had never been made very secure in Egypt; Thebes had its own independent Pharaoh at this time. With the death of Antiochus, who only survived the peace of Apamaea by two years, Ptolemaic preparations for war against the Seleucid kingdom, which was burdened by a heavy tribute, began immediately. The indolent Seleucus IV, who was completely over-shadowed by his powerful, ambitious Chief Minister, Heliodorus, was not a menacing figure, and probably only the death of the Egyptian king prevented the outbreak of hostilities. But the tensions between the last two surviving states that had succeeded to the former Empire of Alexander, obviously sharpened by personal differences between the widowed queen and her brother Seleucus, continued, and there is no doubt that the possession of southern Syria and Palestine was of decisive importance for the ascendancy of either state over the other.

The Jewish community in Jerusalem could not avoid being affected by the events we have just briefly sketched, and even if the appearance of the Seleucids was greeted with joy at first—the long period of Persian rule, which the Seleucids may be considered to have succeeded, will certainly not have been without influence in this—there would be no lack of those who continued to support the Ptolemies. Under the leadership of Joseph the influential Tobiad family, which came originally from Ammonitis perhaps, but which was thoroughly Judaized, had weathered the change of rule extremely well, without severing its connections with the Ptolemies altogether. In view of the statement of Josephus that the Ptolemies had a share in the tax-revenue from former Ptolemaic areas, it is possible that Joseph may have adopted an ambiguous position at first, so that his links with Alexandria were maintained, although he regarded Antiochus as his superior-in-charge. His elder sons, at any rate, allied themselves with the Seleucids to a much greater degree, whereas his youngest son and step-brother, the able and ambitious Hyrcanus, maintained his youthful attachment to Egypt. The uncertain state of the tradition does not allow us to be more definite,[6] but the quarrels which broke out after the death of Joseph between the elder brothers and the youngest step-brother, which at first led to the retreat of Hyrcanus into the country East of the Jordan, were so fierce that they are unintelligible apart from the political situation presupposed by partisanship for the Seleucids or Ptolemies. Moreover, it seems to me worth considering whether there is a hidden connection between the obscure plans of Heliodorus, which obviously aimed at eliminating Seleucus, and the preparations for war at the Egyptian court. Hyrcanus, who was engaged in scuffles with Arabs East of the Jordan, may also have been implicated, in so far as the influence of his brothers in Jerusalem (who had been installed by the Seleucids) could have been broken by a new political grouping, and he might have been able to gain a new position for himself; the exact nature of this position cannot be described, of course, since we do not know what rôle may possibly have been intended for Hyrcanus by the conspiratorial forces. It does not seem at all certain to me that Egypt must have thought of annexing the lost areas with Hyrcanus as Ptolemaic governor; in Alexandria the idea of creating a neutral buffer-state between Syria and Egypt may have seemed an equally feasible alternative; moreover, under the influence of a Ptolemaic supporter such a state would have favoured Egypt, especially since the position of Onias (III)—the high-priest at that time, according to a reliable passage in the Second Book of Maccabees (3.11)—is inconceivable apart from close reference to Hyrcanus and, therefore, the Ptolemies; from this point of view the attitude of Seleucus to Onias and also the action of Antiochus IV in the matter of the High-Priesthood is more intelligible. There is no doubt that Jerusalem occupied a more important position in the power politics of those days than one is at first inclined to assume, and this must be connected primarily with the name of Hyrcanus.

One can, therefore, imagine the difficulties which Antiochus IV faced when he began to rule; in view of the very probable contacts between Heliodorus and the Ptolemies and in view of its importance

[6] We are entirely dependent on Josephus, who has left us two different but chronologically consecutive accounts, the extensive Tobiad narrative which is not particularly plausible as regards historical reliability (Ant. xii. 4. 2–9) and the short, objective summary of Hyrcanus' stay in E. Jordan (Ant. xii. 4. 11), which leads on to what happened under Antiochus Epiphanes and inspires much greater confidence; for details see my article, 'Hyrkan im Ostjordanland', *ZDPV* 71 no. 1 (1955), pp. 70f.

as a buffer-state, his attention was directed primarily to Palestine. But this was bound to bring him into conflict with Egypt, which could hardly tolerate the loss of Palestine and which, even if not held in particularly high esteem at the moment, had always been an ally of Rome; open conflict with Egypt on the part of Antiochus would have been interpreted—justifiably!—as breaking the peace-treaty of Apamaea and would almost certainly have resulted in Roman intervention. But a war with Rome was to be avoided, especially since Demetrius, the son of Seleucus IV, was still being held hostage in Rome, and would have been played off against him. In view of all this we are probably justified in assuming that the relation of Antiochus to the Jewish community was determined in the first instance, at any rate, by political considerations. The fact that in the course of time other motives of a financial and ideological nature assumed prominence should certainly not be denied or underestimated; but action of this nature would have been inconceivable without encouragement from the Jewish side. In fact, in view of the plans of Hyrcanus it is conceivable that the circles which had enlisted in support of the Seleucids in Jerusalem, especially the Tobiad family, were concerned to dispel the hesitations of the new ruler and, by means of a 'Hellenistic' statement of belief, to present him with the spectacle of a politically reliable Jerusalem; it should be added that these circles were not originally rooted in legalistic Judaism and they had long since fallen victim to the influence of Hellenism.

Antiochus obviously found it very convenient that even before he began to rule something had happened which favoured discreet acceptance of the situation in Jerusalem. The High Priest referred to above, Onias III, had gone to the king, even while Seleucus was ruler, in order to lay his complaint personally; he had been unlawfully arrested and sent into asylum at Daphne; we need not concern ourselves at this point with the reasons which led to his exclusion from office. At any rate, when Antiochus came to power, the position of High Priest was vacant. In view of the precarious position of the High Priesthood—representative of the Jerusalem community in relation to the Seleucid government by virtue of its chief position and at the same time responsible for the loyal behaviour of Jerusalem society—the king was extremely interested in the new appointment at a time of such political tension. He avoided the usual hereditary succession and designated as High Priest an influential personality within the Hellenistic faction, who had promised him not only a large sum of money but also pointed to the prospect of establishing a Hellenistic movement of 'Antiochenes', for which purpose he obtained the king's permission to set up a gymnasium in Jerusalem (1 Macc. i. 12–15; 2 Macc. iv. 7f.). There is no need to go into further details, since our concern is to inquire into the causes which probably lie behind Antiochus' action; these are probably to be sought, in fact, primarily in the political situation. Bickermann has described the further actions of the king very graphically and in great detail: these began with his not altogether unjustifiable interference in the question of the High Priesthood, an action which was supported by the Hellenistic party of the Jews by the establishment of an Antiochene 'corporation'; they led to the humiliation of Jerusalem, in that a Hellenistic city-state, 'Acra', replaced the former city, and they finally culminated in the prohibition of the Jewish cult, which thus as it were annulled both the work of Nehemiah and the later work of Ezra. It may be reflected that this last action, which provoked the resistance of the Maccabees and the 'Pious', hardly possessed such importance for Antiochus as is understandably ascribed to it in Biblical and Jewish tradition; for the king it was simply the natural consequence of his previous step, namely the humiliation of Jerusalem. Once Acra had taken the place of Jerusalem and the former Temple of Jerusalem had become the shrine of Acra, a change must have come over the Temple, corresponding to its position as the cult-place of a Hellenistic city-state and a mixed population of Seleucid colonists and Jewish Hellenists. This led to the prohibition of the Jewish cult and then, at first gradually, to the resistance of the Maccabees, whose opposition was strengthened by the support of the 'Pious', obviously by that time a hard and fast group.[7] It is this group that merits our special attention.

In the context of this historical résumé brief reference should be made—it will be discussed in detail later—to the fact that this group of *Hasidim* must have adopted a different attitude from the Maccabean movement in political questions. The details of the alliance of these two opposition groups are no longer very clear. In 1 Macc. ii. 42 it is briefly mentioned that the community of the *Hasidim* were among those who had joined the Maccabees because of the persecution and that their courage and loyalty to the Law were outstanding. A few verses previously (1 Macc. ii. 31–38) there is a description of an attack on Jews who were faithful to the Law; they offered no resistance on the Sabbath for religious reasons and without exception they were all cut down. Thereupon the Maccabees decided to

[7] 1 Macc. ii. 42: *sunagōge Asidaiōn*.

suspend the Sabbath law for the period of active resistance, and it is probably not by chance that it is only after this that reference is made to the 'Pious' joining the Maccabees. 1 Macc. ii. 31f. and ii. 42, therefore, most probably concerned the same group, who, perplexed by the claims of passive and active resistance, found a greater freedom of action only as a result of the Maccabean decision to suspend the Sabbath law. It should also be noted that in the dying testament of Mattathias (1 Macc. ii. 49–68) there is a brief reference (v. 67) to something which is related in greater detail by Josephus (Ant. xii. 6.3), although he says nothing of an alliance of the *Hasidim*, namely the advice of the dying priest that all those faithful to the Law should rally together and strengthen their own ranks. It may be assumed that in following out this advice the Maccabeans will have had to exert no small pressure to persuade the *Hasidim* of the form of active resistance they thought necessary. The attitude of the *Hasidim* at the beginning of the insurrection was similar to that after the edict of restitution which sought to put an official end to the conflict on the death of Antiochus Epiphanes.[8] Alcimus (Jakim), the new High Priest, chosen to act as mediator, seems to have been acceptable to the *Hasidim*, but Judas and his followers continued the armed resistance. In view of this cleavage within the anti-Hellenistic opposition the account of the first Book of Maccabees, which was pro-Hasmonaean in sympathy, is understandably very cautious. It refers to a group of scribes (1 Macc. vii. 12: *sunagōge grammateōn*) and the 'Pious' as if they were two different groups that were particularly relieved at the ending of the conflict and the restoration of peace. This may be a reference to scribes who were perhaps commissioned by the *Hasidim* to test the legitimacy of the new High Priest (cf. v. 14), or it may mean that they themselves were *Hasidim*. The equation of the *Hasidim* with the Maccabean movement[9] in 2 Macc. xiv. 6 may refer to an earlier period of united resistance or—which is equally probable—the passage may be dealing not only with a split between the 'Pious' and the Maccabees but with a division within the *Hasidim*; as a result of their previous alliance in time of war and emergency one section of the *Hasidim* probably became more closely connected with the Maccabees and finally merged into the Maccabean movement;

---

[8] Mentioned briefly by Josephus (Ant. xii. 9. 7) and 1 Macc. vi. 58–59; a more detailed account is given in 2 Macc. xi. 22–26; cf. K. Galling, *Textbuch zur Geschichte Israels*, no. 50 (1950), pp. 79f.

[9] 2 Macc. xiv. 6: *hoi legomenoi tōn Ioudaiōn Asidaioi, hōn aphēgeitai Ioudas ho Makkabaios* . . . .

another section, which may have been led by the scribes referred to above, probably returned to its previous position, after the *status confessionis* came to an end in their eyes. There is a great deal in favour of the hypothesis that in the further course of events, in opposition to the political restoration of the Maccabees, additional splinter groups broke away from this second section; to describe them we have at our disposal only general terms, such as Essenes and Pharisees, which belong to a later period; the present context is not the place to pursue their history further. The original reluctance of the *Hasidim*, however, to take part in armed resistance, and their swift reversal to a policy of waiting passivity, as was apparent during the negotiations, can, in view of the religious courage displayed by the 'Pious', only be explained in terms of a fundamental renunciation of every political tie. In some ways this attitude is reminiscent of that once demanded by Isaiah—to trust in Yahweh and wait with faith; in general, we shall have to ask whether the spiritual outlook of this Hasidic movement was not substantially moulded by elements in the traditions of earlier prophecy. In view of the hopeless condition of our sources there is not much that can be said about this. If, however, we do make the attempt, we can only do so by connecting certain traditions of late Old Testament literature with this Hasidic position. The Book of Daniel is particularly important in this respect.

B

CHAPTER II

THE BOOK OF DANIEL

In the concluding sentences of his commentary on Daniel, Bentzen contrasts the activism of the Maccabees with the preaching of the apocalyptist, whose task it was to foster ' "ideological resistance", the "moral re-armament" of Israel, without which no material preparations could be effective. Whereas the Maccabees strengthened political Messianism, Daniel worked for a position which prepared the way for the Christian attitude, embodied in Jesus, who, following Isa. liii, interpreted the mission of the Son of Man in terms of atoning, redemptive death.'[1] It is perhaps with slight misgiving that one reads such a modern-sounding description of the ideological task of the apocalyptist; but there is no doubt that the various tendencies within the anti-Hellenistic opposition are accurately observed, although there is no attempt on Bentzen's part to link directly the attitude of the apocalyptist and the position of the 'Pious' referred to briefly above. This step has been taken by Noth, however, in his attempt to give a sharper profile to the somewhat pale and colourless appearance of the Hasidic movement.[2] We shall not go into all the numerous questions which the Book of Daniel has posed scholars or discuss the voluminous literature which this book has evoked, but will restrict ourselves to a few observations pertinent to the following study.[3]

Commentaries on the Book of Daniel are almost unanimous in distinguishing between the legends or narratives of the first part and the visions of the second part. There is also general agreement that the legends may be regarded as stemming from the pre-Maccabean period, whereas the cycle of visions is assigned to the final years of the reign of the Seleucid king Antiochus IV Epiphanes, although the book itself, as the occasional dates make clear, purposely seeks to emphasize a certain simultaneity between the events pictured in the narratives and the future events concealed in the visions. It is not

[1] A. Bentzen, *Daniel*, HAT I, no. 19 (1952²), p. 87.
[2] M. Noth, *The History of Israel*, pp. 395ff.
[3] For a full discussion of the questions which are connected with the Book of Daniel, I would refer the reader to my commentary. Here it may simply be noted that to understand the Book of Daniel requires closer attention to its present form than is generally given, even if one is not so convinced of its literary unity as is Rowley, for instance (H. H. Rowley, *HUCA* 23 no. 1 (1950–1), pp. 233–73).

overlooked that the collection of legends in our present Book of Daniel had a history of their own before they reached their present position and that they underwent numerous later additions. Reference has frequently been made to the close connection between ch. ii, which forms part of the narrative, and ch. vii, which in spite of the linguistic difference has good right to be regarded as the prelude to the series of visions.[4] Not only do matching glosses appear to have been worked into both chapters, in order to create the link with the time of Antiochus,[5] but the form and content of both chapters also point to a fairly close relationship, even if the differences should not be underestimated. It can, at any rate, be accepted that ch. ii should be connected more closely with ch. vii than with the other narratives of the first part, and the attempts of Hölscher, Noth etc. to separate a pre-Maccabean kernel in ch. vii also seek to take account of this close connection between ch. vii and one of the chapters belonging to the legend-collection. Also in favour of such a connection is the fact that the visions in ch. vii–xii, like Nebuchadnezzar's dream in ch. ii, are dated, whereas ch. iii–vi, the remaining chapters of the legend-collection, are not so dated.[6] It may, of course, be objected that following the style of prophetic oracles only the visions which were felt to be important have been supplied with a date; but, if that were so, one would expect Nebuchadnezzar's dream in ch. iv to be dated reliably, since formally, at any rate, there is no noticeable difference between the two dreams of Nebuchadnezzar in ch. ii and iv; even in comparison with ch. vii the dream experiences of the

---

[4] On the connection of Dan. ii and vii cf. M. Noth, 'The Understanding of History in Old Testament Apocalyptic' in *The Laws in the Pentateuch and Other Essays* (1966), p. 196. But Noth's observation, correct in itself, that Dan. vii comes from a later period than Dan. ii and has been appended to the collection of legends later (p. 208), can easily lead to misunderstanding; for the visions which follow in Dan. viiif. might also then be regarded as additions. The truth is rather that ch. vii, which has been appended to the Daniel narratives, is at the same time the prelude to the series of visions in ch. vii–xii, so that ch. vii, which looks back to ch. ii, finds its fulfilment in ch. xii, and in this sense may be regarded as the centre of our present Book of Daniel.

[5] In view of the clauses to be excised, especially in the vision of the Son of Man in ch. vii, interpretations diverge widely; cf. for instance G. Hölscher, 'Die Entstehung des Buches Daniel', *TSK*, 92 (1919), pp. 113f., and the even more extensive excisions in M. Noth, 'Zur Komposition des Buches Daniel', *TSK*, 98–99 (1926), pp. 143f., to mention but two divergent views. On the literary unity of the chapter cf. also W. Baumgartner, 'Ein Vierteljahrhundert Danielforschung', *ThR*, N.F. (1939), pp. 59–83, 125–44, 201–8.

[6] In contrast to the stereotyped dating in ch. vii–xii (sometimes in the first, sometimes in the third year of the ruling monarch) the number in ch. ii is unusual; nor can it easily be reconciled with the dating in i. 15, 18 (cf. BH³ *loc. cit.*; Hölscher, p. 118; Bentzen, *loc. cit.*). Emendation may be attempted, but the occurrence of the date can scarcely be eliminated.

Gentile king cannot be considered inferior in quality.[7] In view of the fact that only the night visions of Daniel have been dated and in view of the thematic relationship between ch. ii and vii, the striking dating of ch. ii should be understood in the light of the circumstance that it concerns not only a dream of the Gentile king but also a night vision which comes to Daniel after v. 19. Yet v. 19, together with the two preceding verses 17 and 18 (which contain a reference to the three friends of Daniel named in ch. i), is generally omitted as a secondary addition,[8] even when there is no attempt to eliminate the whole passage ii. 13–18, as Hölscher did, in view of the contradiction between vv. 16 and 25.[9] Moreover, there are also slight inconsistencies in ii. 27–30. In this connection the following considerations seem to me important: in ch. iv, Nebuchadnezzar narrates a dream which affects him personally and as a result of which (in view of the equivalence of ruler and dominion) his kingdom is also involved in misfortune, and requires of his dream-interpreters and Daniel simply the explanation of the dream. In contrast, ch. ii poses the much more difficult task of narrating the dream as well as interpreting it. There is no doubt that the various narratives which make up the first part of the Book of Daniel were originally independent and were only connected later, so that no far-reaching conclusions should be drawn from such comparisons and contradictions. Moreover, the extra dream-sequence in ch. ii was a welcome alteration, since a later collection of legends did, in fact, contain two dreams of Nebuchadnezzar;[10] moreover, it also allowed the superiority of Daniel to his Gentile colleagues to be portrayed more effectively. It should be observed, however, that the more difficult task which the interpreters are set in ch. ii, namely to tell the king both the dream and its interpretation, comes before the lighter task of ch. iv, in which the dream itself is narrated by the king and only the interpretation of it is required; it would be more

---

[7] Ehrlich, 'Der Traum im AT', *BZAW* 73 (1953), p. 102, who appeals to Montgomery, rightly notes that possible differences in the nomenclature, such as dream or night-vision, are to be regarded as depending less on the content of what is seen than on the person of the seer or dreamer.

[8] Likewise the concluding v. 49; cf. C. Kuhl, 'Die drei Männer im Feuer, Daniel 3 und seine Zusätze', *BZAW* 55 (1930), p. 37; the fact that in v. 17 the friends are called by their Hebrew names, whereas in v. 49 their Baylonian names reappear, is understandable; v. 17 looks back to ch. i, which was written in Hebrew, whereas v. 49 introduces ch. iii which is written in Aramaic.

[9] *TSK* 92, pp. 117f.

[10] The suggestion of earlier commenators (cf. Bentzen, p. 45, for literature) that the story of the 'madness' of Nebuchadnezzar in Dan. iii. 31–iv. 34 should be connected with King Nabunaid (Nabonidus) seems to be confirmed by a fragment of the Dead Sea Scrolls (cf. J. T. Milik, 'Prière de Nabonide', *RB* (1956), pp. 407–15).

illuminating if ch. iv preceded ch. ii. What is the explanation of this
slight awkwardness? In contrast to ch. iv the dream in ch. ii does
not contain anything that affects only the king; it seeks to communi-
cate what will happen at the end of days (v. 28f.). In fact, the connection with Israel is not explicitly stated, although it is hinted at,
insofar as the idea of world-history expiring and hastening to its end
in the form of four kingdoms begins with the ruler who has caused
the people of God to lose its political independence. In view of the
night-vision in ch. vii, which takes up the theme of ch. ii again in
another way—this time with stronger reference to Israel, it was
obviously felt necessary to link the visionary of ch. vii more closely
with the dream of Nebuchadnezzar in ch. ii; this seems to be indicated by the fact that Daniel has been made to share the dream of
the king in a night-vision.[11] In this way a certain mounting of tension
between the two formally and thematically related chapters was
attained. The dream of the Gentile king (ch. ii) can be interpreted
by the seer of God's people who has the same dream in a vision of
his own; but his own vision in ch. vii, which is more closely related
to Israel by the figure of the 'Son of Man', has to be explained to
him by a messenger of the heavenly world in view of its importance.
Once again the author of the present book of Daniel seems to have
provided a similar example—in a somewhat different form—of an
intentional climax obtained by means of a reference back to an older
tradition of the narrative section.

As already mentioned, the individual component parts of the
narrative section seem to have possessed a certain degree of independence originally; but ch. iv and v seem to have been linked together
at a very early stage. Not only does ch. v contain express reference
to the facts of ch. iv, but the temporary withdrawal of authority and
power to rule in ch. iv points to a provisional goal that is reached in
ch. v; the rule of the Chaldaeans is overthrown and replaced by that
of the Medes.[12] In ch. v this imminent change of rule is announced

---

[11] Originally the king's demand to know both dream and interpretation (ch. ii)
may have represented an attempt to test his experts (so Bentzen, Ehrlich etc.);
but I cannot escape the impression that the present narrative is at least implying
that the king is feigning a knowledge which he no longer possesses, in fact, because
here—in contrast to ch. iv—is an issue that goes beyond the personal situation of
the king and belongs to the competence of the seer who is particularly receptive
to such situations.
[12] The reader coming from ch. ii is naturally given the impression—undoubtedly
deliberately so—that the point at issue is not so much the overthrow of a kingdom
as a change of dynasty within a kingdom that is depicted as relatively united in
its opposition to the coming rule of God. As is well known ch. vii does not describe
the continuity of the several kingdoms so clearly as ch. ii; but in that the animals

by the visible but illegible and at first inexplicable writing on the wall
of the king's palace; only Daniel can decipher the puzzling writing.
This suggests a certain analogy to ch. ii: the reading and explanation
of the mysterious writing in ch. v may well correspond to the narra-
tion and interpretation of the dream in ch. ii; and the increased
requirements of ch. ii in comparison with the task set in ch. iv may
have been taken from ch. v and been worked into ch. ii by the author
of the present Book of Daniel at a later stage. There is one chapter
within the cycle of visions which stands somewhat to one side and
which cannot be regarded as a vision, but in the middle of which
there is another puzzling message, not this time on 'Gentile territory'
as in ch. v, but a prophetic word of God, meant for Israel and applicable to Israel concerning the seventy years' duration of the exile
and the destruction of Jerusalem (Dan. ix; cf. Jer. xxv. 11; xxix. 10;
Zech. i. 12; 2 Chron. xxxvi. 21).[13] The wise interpreter of the
puzzling writing of ch. v fails, just as the wise dream-interpreter of
ch. iv had failed in the face of his own vision in ch. vii. Once again
intervention from the divine world was required for him to understand the prophetic word in ch. ix. Is it mistaken to assume that this
connection is deliberately contrived and that the use of certain motifs
from older traditions is intended to emphasize what was or was felt
to be more important? Divine revelations which manifest themselves
in dream (ch. iv) or riddle (ch. v) in the Gentile world and are
primarily concerned with the fate of Gentile kingdoms and their
rulers, as in the old Daniel narratives, are interpreted by Daniel,
the seer, himself; but he himself stands in need of inspiration from
the divine world, when the vision is directed to him (ch. vii) or the
word of God to be interpreted is derived from Israel's sphere of
revelation (ch. ix) and thus relates primarily to the fate of the people
of God, as in the visions of the Book of Daniel. It may be remarked
in passing that the interpreter of a revealed prophetic word also

---

[13] The prayer of Daniel in ix. 4–20 may be regarded as a secondary insertion;
but this is hardly true of all ch. ix, which is intended as a transition from the vision
in ch. viii to the vision in ch. x–xii, in order to emphasize the significance of the
final vision.

---

are contrasted with the figure of the 'Son of Man' this continuity is perhaps taken
into consideration. But the chronology of ch. vii deserves special attention, in my
opinion. The 'Son of Man'-vision is dated to the first year of the ruler, who ceased
to rule at the same time that the change from 'golden' to 'silver' kingdom took
place; the purpose of this was probably to point to the finality of the end discussed
in ch. vii; but cf. M. Noth, 'The Understanding of History in Old Testament
Apocalyptic' in *The Laws in the Pentateuch and Other Essays* (1966), p. 209, who
attributes no significance to the dating of the 'Son of Man' vision.

requires inspiration from the divine world; this points to a continuity
between the earlier prophet and the later interpreter. Ch. ii occupies
a central position in that it is concerned with a dream stemming
from the Gentile world, the dream of a Gentile king, in fact, but, at
the same time, is concerned with a message which has the end of
the world in view and is, therefore, also concerned with Israel
indirectly. The author of the present Book of Daniel has taken this
into account, in that in ch. ii he involves the seer of God's people
in the dream of the Gentile king by a vision of his own. He felt
himself compelled to do this, because he was indebted to the old
tradition of ch. ii for important ideas for the message which he had
now to deliver to his people. He made use of the old kernel of ch. ii
as a thematic introduction to his book, and by means of the vision of
Daniel which he inserted he gave to the old story of the Gentile
king's dream something of the character of the visions which he
appended later. Thus, the present ch. ii, which serves as a thematic
introduction, is a combination of the two types of material found in
the Book of Daniel, the narratives of the first part and the visions
of the second. The author has attached to this introduction the
tradition of the three men in the fire (ch. iii), whom he had introduced
in the preface (ch. i) as friends of Daniel. It would not have been
difficult to have made Daniel the main hero of the story in ch. iii
also; but after the brilliant performance of Daniel in ch. ii, ch. iii
would not have made sense with Nebuchadnezzar and Daniel as the
central figures. He let ch. iii follow ch. ii, however, probably because
apart from other reasons he found a slender connection between the
statues in the dream of the Gentile king and the cult image which
Nebuchadnezzar had erected (ch. iii): in view of what was reported
in ch. ii about the end of the empire symbolized in the statue the
three devout men did right in refusing to worship the cult image of
the king. Sapienti sat! The most important parts of the narratives
which he took over he was able to leave untouched, particularly
ch. iv and v which belonged together; but he altered the chronological
sequence by placing the 'Son of Man' vision (ch. vii), which was
dated to the first year of Belshazzar's reign, later than the events
recorded in ch. vi, which took place, in fact, under Darius the Mede,
the *successor* of Belshazzar![14] He did not want to destroy the close
connection between ch. iv and v, which he would have had to do if
he had placed ch. vii where it chronologically belonged, namely at

---

[14] There is no need to go into the historical and genealogical inaccuracies in
the order of the various rulers more closely at this point.

the beginning of Belshazzar's reign; nor did he want to interrupt the series of visions beginning with ch. vii by adopting a later position for ch. vi, which took place in the reign of Darius. Moreover, he may have seen a hidden connection between the lions in ch. vi and the first animal in the vision of ch. vii—similar to the correspondence between ch. ii and iii noted above. In this way, then, he succeeds in linking the events on earth, as described in the narrative sections, and the events of the future, as revealed in visions to the seer, more closely together.

Numerous questions remain, but they do not need to be discussed in the present context. Here it must suffice to point out that there is a much closer connection, quite deliberately contrived, between the narratives and the visions of the Book of Daniel than is usually assumed. At any rate, the author of the visions seems to have derived important ideas from the old narrative collection, such as the concept of world-history in the form of four world-empires with its eschato-logical-theocentric conclusion. This gave him the possibility not only of legitimating the Daniel of the visions by the Daniel of the narratives and thus obtaining greater credence for the eschatological message of the seer, but also of clothing the Daniel of the visions with a greater dignity in accordance with the importance of his visionary communications. Daniel's great knowledge as interpreter of dreams is undoubtedly a special gift of the God of Israel; but it still remains within the range of what might be expected from a Gentile interpreter of dreams. But because the dreams of the Gentile king have been inspired by the God of Israel they can only be inter-preted by the seer of Israel who has been specially equipped for this. A much higher value, however, is to be set on Daniel's eschatological knowledge, which no longer simply rests on a talent bestowed on him by God but has been mediated to him directly by a messenger from the divine world. Thus, behind the connection of the narratives with the visions lies a well-thought-out plan, which is not without significance for the understanding of the Book of Daniel as a whole.

Of course, the difference between the wisdom of the dream-interpreter and the wisdom of the apocalyptic seer is also preserved by the fact that the wisdom of the dream-interpreter, a talent be-stowed on him by God, continues to be linked specifically with him. It may indeed serve to confirm and strengthen faith, in that it lifts man's gaze to the God of Israel, who is able to bestow such gifts on members of his people. The wisdom of the seer, however, hastens to be recognized and accepted by men, and those who are illuminated by it are those who in xi. 33 are called 'the wise men of the people', who—following Isa. liii—help many to insight, patiently suffer martyrdom (xi. 33, 35), but will one day shine like the stars (xii. 3). There can be no doubt which sort of wisdom is being thought of here. It is the wisdom of the apocalyptist, the knowledge that the events foreseen by the visionary and now commencing are hastening to their fulfilment, since what was predetermined is being carried into effect, and, what is more, this is happening, as was programmatically announced in ii. 34, 35 and was re-emphasized in viii. 25, without any intervention by the hand of man. The fact that the military action of the Maccabees is described as 'little help' (xi. 34) and that it was not accepted without misgiving in view of this theocentric expectation has been noted often enough and has recently been rightly emphasized once more by Bentzen. The passive but loyal attitude displayed by the Book of Daniel agrees well with the position of the *Hasidim* indicated in 1 Macc. ii. It would be common knowledge that under persecution different groups had come together in order to avert the direct invasion of the Hellenistic spirit and preserve their ancestral heritage, but, as is often the case with opposition-groups, had been motivated by different impulses in the theological reasons they gave for their common venture. They did, of course, share important convictions of faith, to mention but the belief in personal resurrection, which sprang into prominence during the persecution and which we shall have to discuss in connection with the Book of Daniel; but the differences, which are equally clear, reveal a fairly powerful cleavage within the opposition movement. One of the most substantial points of cleavage probably lies in the different evaluation of events at that time. The fact that Dan. xii. 1 knows of no historical parallel, since men dwelt on earth, to the period of oppression now beginning, may be insignificant, but it may elucidate the cleavage within the anti-Hellenistic opposition; there are no analogies for the events now taking place, because the onset of the eschatological time is at issue; the significance of this for Israel is briefly referred to in Dan. xii. 1–3. The first Book of Maccabees does not deny the severity of this critical period; but the time reference in 1 Macc. ix. 27 shows that it does not fall outside the framework of previous history: it is a period of oppression, the like of which has not been seen in Israel since the period of the prophets came to an end. It is, however, a chronological description, to which it is not necessary to attach any eschatological interpretation directly; despite all tribulations, it remains one period of time among others, and its troubles can be overcome by courageous and loyal faith. Thus, the activism of the Maccabees and the succeeding struggle for power waged by Judas and the political restoration which assumed an increasingly definite profile were ultimately based on a non-eschatological understanding of events connected with the Seleucids. This poses the question, therefore: did such a non-eschatological interpretation have an antecedent history like the eschatological expectation of the *Hasidim*?

Even the beliefs which were held in common by the two opposition groups, such as the expectation of a personal resurrection, for instance, reveal slight differences. Piety shaped by the Maccabean movement had neither the desire nor the ability to reject this new element of faith. If we may adduce the second Book of Maccabees,[15] although at some points it obviously reflects the view of other groups, to describe this piety, we see that belief in resurrection is closely connected with loyalty to the Law; loyalty in the sense of martyrdom (ch. vii) occupies a prominent position—understandably at a time of persecution, although it may certainly be understood in the sense of a more general observance of the Law, without necessity of martyrdom. The Gentile king, however, is denied all hope of resurrection (vii. 14). Dan. xii. 2 also knows no universal resurrection, for it refers only to 'many' who go to meet the resurrection; the Gentile world is obviously not included.[16] At the same time Dan. xii refers to a double resurrection, for some to eternal life, for others to eternal shame. The fact that the wise are mentioned as a third group may be left out of account, to begin with; they undoubtedly belong to

---

[15] In the first instance it is ch. vii and xii (xii. 39f) that come in question; common to both chapters is the close connection of martyrdom and resurrection. Chapter xii is important in that it gives two reasons for the preparation of an atoning sacrifice—for slain Maccabean party members, in fact, who have been found with Gentile amulets in their possession. The first reason (xii. 42) requires an expiatory sacrifice in order that the Maccabean movement as a whole might not suffer because of the transgression of individuals who have been slain, whereas the second reason (xii. 43) argues from the resurrection that warriors who have fallen in war for a good cause should not be deprived of resurrection in spite of their transgression. The absence of a form-critical study of the two Books of Maccabees is very regrettable. Their diverse origins are undisputed; nevertheless, there will be no great desire to link 2 Macc. too closely with the Hasidic movement. K. D. Schunck, *Die Quellen des 1 und 2 Makkabäerbuches* (Diss. Greifswald, 1954) shows that a great deal depends on one's estimate of the texts used in the two books.

[16] The translation of (*ha*)*rabbim* as 'multitude', 'all'. advocated by J. Jeremias, *Die Abendmahlsworte Jesu* (1949[2]), pp. 91–93, 108–11; *ThWB* 6, pp. 536f., is not being disputed; but, as the use of (*ha*)*rabbim* in the writings of the Qumran community (cf. the Damascus Document) shows, the inclusive interpretation refers to the totality of a community, which deliberately sets out to separate itself from the rest of mankind or other communities; hence, it should not be overlooked that a point of cleavage may lie alongside the stress on inclusion.

the first group, but are mentioned separately for a special reason. But this double resurrection, which is not immediately intelligible, has probably only one meaning, when it is connected exclusively with Israel. Without denying influences and additions from foreign religions, which undoubtedly promoted the growth and extension of belief in the resurrection, the revival of the people of God, as portrayed in Ezek. xxxvii, for instance, is, within the ideas of the Old Testament, primarily an eschatological hope, which could now only be applied to themselves in the sense of a personal-individual expectation by those who were convinced by the eschatological understanding of the present as the last time. This indicates the cleft which had begun to divide the Jewish community, which was based on cult and law. It originated, so far as we have been able to trace, when, as a result of Hellenization, the cleavage between those who were loyal to the Law and those who scorned the covenant was already a frightening reality. The idea of a double resurrection was necessary because the prophetic hope of Israel's restoration applied to the whole people of God but in the sense of a resurrection to life was to be expected only by those who were prepared to register their own decision for the ancestral faith and who by reason of this personal decision could also be assured of a personal reward in the sense of resurrection to life; the others were not excluded from resurrection but could only expect resurrection to eternal shame. This cleavage was still further deepened when with the expiration of passive and active resistance the different motives of the opposition could no longer be concealed. Hence in Dan. xii. 3 the wise receive special emphasis, in order to make clear that only in laying claim to the eschatological interpretation taught by these wise was there to be found the exclusive and distinctive sign of the people of the 'Saints of the Most High', i.e., membership of the true Israel. In various places the first Book of Maccabees also unhesitatingly identifies the aim of the Maccabean movement with the fact of Israel (cf. iii. 10; viii. 18; ix. 27 etc.); but, once in power, the Maccabean movement, like a political party, was able to show greater tolerance and to limit the conditions for membership in the state of Israel to acceptance of the Maccabean state and a formal observance of the law within the framework of this new state. The Book of Daniel, however, reveals the conventicle-spirit of deliberate separatism in that membership of the 'true' Israel is made to depend on the acknowledgement of a certain dogma, namely the eschatological interpretation of historical events, which meant, in effect, membership of a particular group.

Understandably during the period of persecution these distinctions are still very fluid at first; they take clearer shape, however, with the emergence of the compromise high-priest Alcimus, when the intention of the Maccabees to fight for power becomes more obvious. The separation is not from the enemy but from the former ally, and in the following years and decades it will lead to the fierce conflicts between the Hasmonaeans and the Pharisees and to the monastic isolation of the Essenes, both of which groups may justifiably be regarded as successors of the former *Hasidim*. Initial traces of this splintering can be discerned in the Book of Daniel. This is the reason for our examination of the probable pressupositions of an earlier epoch which have culminated in such a division; for it is to be assumed that the Book of Daniel stands at the end of a historical development, as well as introducing a new period in the religious history of Judaism.

In this connection, therefore, further reference may be permitted to Dan. vii. We have already linked ch. vii fairly closely with ch. ii, and we may do the same now with ch. vii and ch. xii, because we regard ch. vii as the keystone of the whole Book of Daniel. The visions following ch. vii in ch. viii–xii are then to be understood as a gradual progressive development of what has already been introduced in broad outline in ch. vii. But whoever may be meant by 'Son of Man' in the vision and the 'Holy Ones' or 'Saints of the Most High' or 'the people of the Saints of the Most High' in the interpretation of the vision, namely the one(s) who are given the power to rule, the visions of ch. viiif., which develop the vision of ch. vii, fail to explain this not unimportant feature of a transfer of rule; such an explanation must be contained, if at all, in the introductory verses of ch. xii, so that the transfer of world-dominion is presented in the form of a personal resurrection, i.e., in the sense of an individual application of the restoration of Israel, which was, of course, originally meant to be collective. It is not absolutely clear, however, what the terms 'Holy Ones', 'Saints of the Most High', 'People of the Saints of the Most High' in Dan. vii represent; at any rate, there is no proof that it refers directly to the Jewish state. Recently M. Noth[17] has revived the view proposed by Mowinckel and Procksch, 'that in the main body of Dan. vii the Saints of the Most High refer to the heavenly hosts of God, that only later did a change of reference'—namely to Israel—'take place, and that the

[17] *Interpretationes ad Vetus Testamentum pertinentes Sigmundo Mowinckel septuagenario missae* (1955), pp. 146–161; *The Laws in the Pentateuch and Other Essays*, pp. 215–8.

statement of S. Mowinckel, that the Holy Ones in the Old Testament were divine beings, is confirmed by Dan. vii . . .' (p. 158). Noth's conclusion seems inescapable, in view of the passages he cites not only from the Old Testament but also from the Damascus Document and from the Dead Sea Scrolls discovered up to that date. One must also agree with Noth that the verses which clearly emphasize the identity of the 'Holy Ones' with Israel (vii. 21f.) may contain secondary expansion, even if one is not inclined, as Noth is, to assume a fairly long antecedent history for Dan. vii, but would rather derive the chapter from the early period of Antiochus IV with the addition of explanatory clauses in the course of subsequent discussion.[18] Noth also admits that 'Saints of the Most High' was understood at a very early date to refer to Israel. The only question in my mind is whether the elimination of the only passage which refers expressly to such a connection, a passage which, it is true, is generally accepted as an expansion, does justice to the intentions of the Book of Daniel. In my opinion it would be truer to say that the unexpressed relation of the 'Saints of the Most High' and God's people was one of the presuppositions which provided the foundation for the present Book of Daniel; hence the secondary expansion is not inaccurate. It would be better, however, not to think in terms of a formal identity of the two terms so much as the inclusion of what is understood by Israel throughout the Book of Daniel in the undoubtedly heavenly world of the 'Saints'. It is this which is obviously meant to be expressed in the figure of the 'Son of Man'.[19]

There is widespread agreement in commentaries on the Book of Daniel that the figure and also the precedence of the 'Son of Man' over the animals is meant to illustrate the distinctive position of the people of God in comparison with the rest of the world and its unparalleled relation to the divine world. How this figure of the 'Son of Man' arose may be explained and illustrated by numerous references from the field of comparative religion; but the decisive argument must be taken from the overall structure of the Book of Daniel and the way the separate passages in the book agree. It is

[18] Cf. O. Eissfeldt, *The Old Testament: an Introduction* (1965), pp. 525ff.

[19] Too sharp a distinction between vision and interpretation, therefore, does not seem to me very helpful for the understanding of ch. vii. The conclusion arrived at by Vielhauer, *Gottesreich und Menschensohn, Festschrift für G. Dehn* (1957), pp. 51–79 following Baumgartner, *ThR*, N.F. 11 (1939), pp. 214 f., that the human figure of the vision is not an individual person, but, as the contrast with the animals shows, a symbol for the eschatological kingdom (pp. 72–73), needs supplementing to the extent that the relation of Israel, or what is understood by the term 'Israel' in the Book of Daniel, to this eschatological kingdom is not passed over in silence; in fact, this is what the Book of Daniel is concerned with.

probably the seer himself, transported in his vision into the divine world and participating in the events of the divine world, who provided the model for the figure of the 'Son of Man'. This means, however, that a life and attitude which accord with the knowledge which was communicated to the seer when he was transported into the divine world will lead to reception into the divine world and to participation in the eschatological dominion, in the way already shown in the case of the 'Son of Man'. Apart from other important concerns, this is the purpose of the Book of Daniel in its present form. It is certainly meant to encourage loyalty in times of persecution; equally, it is meant to strengthen the conviction that a divine plan is being brought to fulfilment in the face of the powers of this world, as the prophets had proclaimed, and the rule thus established is to be of eternal duration. Its principal concern, however, is that those members of Israel who have been guided and directed by the knowledge granted to the seer should participate in the coming of this eschatological kingdom. In short, it is concerned with the formation of a conventicle-type force, which is still connected with the empirical Israel but which desires to be considered as the 'true' Israel, separated by the resurrection from the rest of the world and united with the 'Saints of the Most High' as the 'People of the Saints of the Most High'.

The fact that such an interpretation of what is to be understood by 'Israel' can still count on the Maccabean movement as a 'little help' may be an indication that the actual empirical limitation and separation of the eschatological Israel is still quite fluid; but in principle, putting the matter dogmatically, it is determined by acceptance of the interpretation of contemporary events communicated to the seer and proclaimed by him.

This brings us to the questions which we had in mind in undertaking this summary review of the Book of Daniel. The whole structure of the book, the assumption of definite traditions in the narratives of the first section, which are already eschatologically orientated to a certain extent, and the secondary, but not very much later, accretions in ch. vii or in the concluding section ch. xii, make clear that we should probably hold a particular individual responsible for the structure of the Book of Daniel, although this does not therefore mean an individual in the sense of the pre-exilic prophets; it would be more accurate to regard the author as the spokesman of a particular group and of the point of view represented by such a group. If we bring together this group and the *Hasidim*, then we may well ask whether we are dealing with an *ad hoc* alliance which came into being purely as a result of religious conflict, which is not a very probable hypothesis, or whether we can find traces of its earlier history in the previous decades. If so, we should have to consider the possibility that earlier references to the *Hasidim* are hardly to be expected; but the views they represent, as they found expression in the Book of Daniel, can perhaps be traced backwards in spite of certain changes. Not unnaturally the first group of traditions calling for consideration are those stemming from the earlier prophets, so that we must subject late eschatological sections in the writings of the prophets, such as the 'Apocalypse' of Isaiah (Isa. xxiv–xxvii) or the final chapters of the Book of Zechariah, to a somewhat closer analysis; we shall do this in ch. iv. We shall also have to bear in mind that the transition from prophetic eschatology (even in the form it takes in late sections of the prophetic literature) to the apocalyptic eschatology of the Book of Daniel did not occur without a certain break in development. For example, an overt sign of this is the transition from anonymity to pseudonymity. A self-contained unit like Isa. xxiv–xxvii, for instance, has certainly nothing to do with the prophet Isaiah, but as an anonymous composition it was able to find entrance into the prophetic canon, whereas this way was barred to the pseudonymous Book of Daniel. It is true that this is to be explained in the first place by the fact that, according to certain statements in the 'Praise of the Fathers' in Jesus ben Sira, a canon of prophetic writing was already fairly well established about 190 B.C., so that the Book of Daniel which was written later could no longer find a place.[20] But during the preparatory work for the present study I came to regard it as increasingly probable that the gradual collection of the products of the prophetic spirit into a canon parallel to the Pentateuch was not led primarily by the representatives of the official Jewish community; rather,—to express it somewhat vaguely in the first place—it was directed by groups that had a definite eschatological interest and lived on the spirit of prophecy into paths which may perhaps be regarded as an earlier stage of the *Hasidim*. It is in their midst that the viewpoint represented by later Pharisaism probably developed, namely that the prophets were to be understood as tradents and interpreters of the *Torah*, so that the

---

[20] Of the books in the prophetic canon Eccles. xlviii and xlix refers to the twelve Minor Prophets (xlix. 12) as well as Isa., Jer., Ezek., so that about 190 B.C. there may be detected a certain finality in the collection of prophetic writings, although it cannot be determined whether the prophetic writings at that time contained all that is now known to us.

collection of prophetic literature gradually won canonical authority as a supplement to the Pentateuch, at any rate in these circles, whereas other circles of Judaism, such as we can recognise later in the Sadducees, opposed and rejected such a view. The presupposition for such a collection of prophetic traditions on a larger scale (i.e. including the anonymous additions—primarily eschatological in content—made in the course of time) was the view, again developed by these circles with an eschatological interest, regarding the disappearance of the prophetic spirit, which according to later Pharisaism had passed to the scribes.[21] As is well known this view had established itself in another way also and had already, for example, found expression in the first book of Maccabees, where the present is described on three occasions as the period without prophets (iv. 46; ix. 27; xiv. 41). But one has the feeling that these expressions ('. . . since no more prophets have appeared . . .', ix. 27; '. . . until a prophet appear . . .', iv. 46; similarly xiv. 41), which look like descriptions of time, conceal a hidden purpose. Prophecy was widely recognized as a historical phenomenon of the past and its importance was undisputed; the arrival of the eschatological millenium was also associated, perhaps *bona fide*, with an appearance of prophets. But it appears to be used here as a date like the Greek calends, since the present represented by the Maccabean state was certainly not intended to be regarded eschatologically. Originally, however, at any rate in the eschatologically minded circles which re-appear a few years or decades later among the *Hasidim*, the theory of the disappearance of prophecy was essentially the final factor which made possible the collection of prophetic literature so as to be able to give a devotional interpretation of the collected writings and, hence, to live by them. Thus, the gradual preparation of a prophetic canon as a supplement to the *Torah* is to be regarded as a telling appeal to maintain the Law without surrendering the expectation of a millenium.

We shall have to re-examine these reflections, which we have sketched only briefly so far, more fully in the following pages; at this point, in view of the problem of anonymity in certain sections of the prophets and the pseudonymity of the apocalyptic literature, which we have touched on above, we shall simply mention one other final problem that we must keep before our eyes. If the same circles which were responsible for bringing the collection of prophetic writings to a provisional close about the year 200 B.C. were also the

---

[21] Cf. B. Bath. 12a; j. ber. I 3b, 26.

source of the pseudonymous Book of Daniel a few decades later, it would not have been difficult for them to insert the book in the prophetic writings. Omission was probably deliberate. It was realized that the prophetic hopes of restoration applied to an Israel which no longer existed as a result of the cleavage within the Jewish community during the period of religious conflict. Thus, the pseudonymity of the apocalyptic eschatology announces a new Israel, which will not surrender its connection with the earlier Israel, but which represents a new Israel insofar as it forms a part of the expected eschatological rule of God. Analysis of the presuppositions which led to such a development is the object of this study. It seems advisable, therefore, to stress at the outset certain important distinguishing marks between the apocalyptic eschatology we meet in the Book of Daniel, and prophetic eschatology, to link with this reflections on the rise of apocalyptic, and then to analyse the above-mentioned sections in the prophetic writings, in which we may detect earlier traces both of the circles represented by the Book of Daniel and of the view they maintained within the Jewish community in the period up to the appearance of Antiochus IV.

C

CHAPTER III

REFLECTIONS ON THE RISE OF APOCALYPTIC

WE shall introduce the difficult question of the rise of Jewish apocalyptic with some preliminary observations. It is customary to regard the influx of foreign influences, particularly the adoption of the Iranian dualistic cosmology, as responsible for the birth of apocalyptic eschatology. This is certainly true in view of the political situation of the post-exilic community, which was part of the Persian Empire. In addition, one could also refer to the great influence of the Diaspora as the mediator of foreign ideas, both the Diaspora in Babylon during the Persian period and also the Diaspora in Egypt, since Palestine came under Ptolemaic rule for a century about 300 B.C. But the appropriation of foreign concepts, whether by direct or indirect transmission from the Diaspora to the Jewish community in Palestine, presupposes a certain openness, which is not easily reconciled with their recorded attempts to cut themselves off from the world outside, as, in fact, they were encouraged to do by the Babylonian Diaspora. Hence we must take into account the possibility of certain presuppositions within the Jewish community that may explain the ready acceptance and appropriation of foreign ideas.

Such presuppositions must have been formed in the pre-Maccabean period. For if the Book of Daniel presents us with a picture of an apocalyptic expectation, the main lines of which are already fairly fixed, the beginnings of this apparently recent form of eschatology must lie in the pre-Maccabean period. In that case it will hardly serve to elucidate our problem, if we concentrate on those apocalypses transmitted in writing, which, even though they undoubtedly contain old elements of tradition, belong to a later period, at any rate in their written form. But we may perhaps take up with profit an inference which may be drawn from the later apocalypses. In the various statements regarding certain points of the eschatological event, for instance regarding the final judgement, life after death, the figure of the Messiah etc., the apocalyptic writings sometimes diverge widely from one another; yet in spite of these differences there is a constant background of a common world of ideas, a comparatively unified world-view (*Weltanschauung*), more or less clearly recognizable. This tells in favour of a common origin of apocalyptic

ideas; but, at the same time, it is difficult to escape the impression
that, even at the early stage at which we have to surmise apocalyptic
originating, an organizing, unifying hand, such as the tradition of
an office with clearly defined functions, comparable to that which—
despite changes—we can recognize in the priesthood, was missing;
this meant that from the beginning there was plenty of scope for the
future development and differentiation of specific ideas. In contrast
to the fairly unified world of priesthood we are reminded of the
many-sided, differentiated world of prophecy, in which adherence
to a definite tradition and the free, unregimented development of
parts of a tradition, i.e. a creative charisma, are to be found side by
side in a somewhat uneasy relationship. We are suggesting, in fact,
that in the watchful trust of the Book of Daniel and the Hasidic
circles which stand behind it we can recognize an attitude such as
an Isaiah had recommended to his people centuries before.

The connection between prophecy and apocalyptic has never been
seriously disputed, and there is also widespread agreement that this
connection finds embodiment in a common eschatological outlook.
Of course, prophecy was not concerned solely with eschatology;
even apocalyptic seems to pursue a more comprehensive path sometimes, in that it represents a world-view in an eschatological key,
similar to and probably also dependent on a later universal form of
Israelite wisdom. It is not accidental that Daniel the apocalyptist,
who announces the end of this world, is legitimated by Daniel the
wise, while the wisdom of Daniel attains its climax in its knowledge
of the end of this world and the coming rule of God. Even if the
eschatological aspect forms a substantial link between prophecy and
apocalyptic, the obvious differences between prophetic and apocalyptic eschatology cannot be ignored. It will be advisable, therefore, to
recall briefly and epigrammatically the most important differences,
drawing on the opinions of well-known previous works.

Volz, in the introduction to his great work on the eschatology of
the Jewish community in the post-Maccabean period, gave a brief
account of the basic mood of apocalyptic and emphasized the following main points[1]: a religious, deterministic point of view, stemming from the plan of Yahweh proclaimed by the older prophets;
the unity of the world as the enemy of God, embodied in the great
homogeneous empire which is in subjection to the power of evil;
the limitation of human influence in favour of the unilateral activity

---

[1] P. Volz, *Die Eschatologie der jüdischen Gemeinde im neutestamentlichen Zeitalter*
(1934²), p. 4f.

of God in a supernatural, miraculous form, and, connected with this, a strong emphasis on angels and demons; a pessimistic-dualistic view of the world, which resulted in a marked other-worldliness combined with expectation of judgement and individual resurrection. We shall supplement the description of Volz, which is not specifically interested in the difference between prophetic and apocalyptic eschatology, by a much sharper distinction of the two approaches, as Buber does in his open rejection of apocalyptic.[2] In his comparison the following points of difference are emphasized: in contrast to the native, monistic eschatology of prophecy apocalyptic eschatology is foreign—in fact, Iranian in origin—and dualistic; whereas the goal of the prophetic hope is the fulfilment of creation, because evil, in itself directionless, can be guided in the direction of the good by an act of consecration in which man is decisively involved, apocalyptic, in its separation of good and evil, aims at the dissolution and abolition of creation by another, different type of world; it can only despair of this earth as an object of hopeless corruption. Finally, judgement in the prophets is a coming event which is announced when those summoned to repent refuse to do so; but it is—as the example of the prophet Jonah shows—by no means irrevocable. For apocalyptic, however, judgement is an unalterable event, the coming of which is so firmly fixed that its date can be calculated.

Further observations could, of course, be added, as for instance after the manner of the description given by Lindblom[3]; yet, in the main, prophetic eschatology seems clearly distinct from the apocalyptic expectation of the future. Taken in connection with the differences described by Volz, the following contrasts between the two eschatological approaches are all that need be emphasized in the present context: firstly, the monistic or dualistic view of God and the world; secondly, the different aims towards which the creation moves (the fulfilment of creation or its dissolution and replacement by a different type of world); and finally, the different view of judgement—on the one hand, an imminent event, repeatable if necessary, and with a beneficent, propaideutic stress, and, on the other hand, a unique event, an unrepeatable destiny, leading to a *totaliter aliter*.

It will not be out of place to develop this comparison with the help of a further characteristic difference, to which frequent reference has already been made. The eschatological sections in the prophetic

[2] M. Buber, *Kampf um Israel* (1933), pp. 59f.
[3] J. Lindblom, *Die Jesaja-Apokalypse. Jes.* 24–27 (1938), p. 102.

writings are generally suspected of not being genuine. Although this argument may not be absolutely justified, it is true that alterations and expansions in the prophetic literature are particularly strong in eschatological passages; but they are anonymous expansions, which obviously hope to be regarded as consecutive interpretations. The apocalypses are not anonymous, but pseudonymous; in this way they emphasize their independence and do not restrict their pseudonymous products to the specifically prophetic sphere. Alongside apocalypses which claim to stem from prophets like Isaiah or Elijah, there are others which claim to stem from men of the Law, such as Moses or Ezra or the patriarchs or even from figures of grey pre-history, such as Adam and Enoch. One has the impression that in every dimension of Israel's revelation right back to the very beginning of mankind the witnesses worked as witnesses of the apocalyptic world-view. This reveals a completely different type of mentality from that discernible in the anonymous eschatological additions within the prophetic literature, a new type of mentality which can only be explained as a result of a new understanding of what Israel represents in the world. How did this change come about and how can the initial factors which led to this change be traced? They took shape during the period when the structure of Israelite society underwent other momentous changes also, namely the time, almost unparalleled in history, when Israel ceased to be a political state and became a religious community, a theocracy instead of a nation.[4] This change seems to me to have been of particular importance for the metamorphosis of eschatological expectation; it is, therefore, a good place for us to begin.

Even if it is true that in reconstructing a historical or religious development one must treat of broad outlines and be allowed to omit a great deal, it will be necessary to ask for sympathetic understanding in our use of this liberty in the following pages. Primarily, we shall be concerned in broad outline with the understanding of history to be found in the great post-exilic historical works in Israel, in order to derive from them inferences which may help us to answer the problems posed above. It is true that every reconstruction remains hypothetical, especially when there are only a few sources at our disposal; but every hypothesis lives in hope of bringing at least some illumination.

---

[4] Cf. on this M. J. Lagrange, *Le Judaisme avant Jésus-Christ* (1931), pp. 33f.; also E. Auerbach, *Wüste und Gelobtes Land* (1936), pp. 231f., and especially A. Causse, *Du groupe ethnique à la communauté réligieuse* (1937), esp. p. 217.

Rost[5] has tried to prove that the term *kahal yisrael* which was used synonymously with *'am yisrael* in the older period underwent a change of meaning in the time of Hezekiah, especially in Deuteronomy, as a result of theological reflection; the levy of the men of Israel for military or cultic service now became the levy of Yahweh and its scope was extended to include the women also. This change of meaning, however, was not able to establish itself fully, even if it was not without influence in the following period (pp. 7–32). Possibly the term *kahal* was too heavily steeped in tradition for it to undergo a lasting change of meaning. Hence, the Priestly Writing, adhering to the consciously theological meaning of *kahal* and at the same time having regard for the changed political situation, used the term *'edah* to describe the ancient people of God, a term which appears only rarely in documents of the pre-exilic period.[6] The Priestly Writing thus falls back on the personal group-names of the old nomadic period (tribes, father's houses etc.), obviously intending 'to depict a cultically pure religious group' without the political ingredients which appeared with the introduction of kingship. Hence it is obvious that the *'edah* is regarded as the successor the old *'am yisrael*, without all the functions of the *'am* (e.g. military service) being transferred to the *'edah*.

This brief sketch takes no account of the details which Rost investigated in his book; it is only meant to be a starting-point, to be supplemented by an attempt to describe in a few sentences the thematic purpose of the Priestly Writer's narrative as a whole. If Noth is right in his view that the narrative of the Priestly Writing never contained an account of the Conquest, because it was not interested in the Conquest, and that it ended with the tradition of the deaths of Aaron and Moses,[7] then the events on the mount of God, which led to the establishment of the national and cultic community (*Volks- und Kultgemeinde*), did, in fact, embody the goal which the Priestly Writing set out to describe. It is not quite clear, however, why von Rad's view,[8] that the development of the Priestly narrative is marked by three concentric circles, relating to Adam,

[5] L. Rost, *Die Vorstufen von Kirche und Synagoge im Alten Testament*, BWANT IV no. 24 (1938).

[6] Details in Rost, *op cit.*, pp. 32f.

[7] M. Noth, *Überlieferungsgeschichtliche Studien* I (1938), pp. 206f.

[8] G. v. Rad, *Die Priesterschrift im Hexateuch*, BWANT, IV no. 13 (1934), pp. 166f. The present work was finished in the summer of 1957 and has been in my hands for only a few days since then, so that it has not been possible to make detailed references to works which have appeared since; I regret this especially in the case of v. Rad's *Theology of the Old Testament I-II*.

Noah and Abraham, cannot be harmonized with this. His conclusion, however, that the idea of covenant was no longer important in the Priestly Writing is too sweeping. Undoubtedly, the Priestly Writing freed the idea of the covenant from older presentations of it and shaped it more freely, but not by violating existing traditions so that the work fell apart; rather, because it offered the possibility of taking over the universal outlook of the Yahwist's historical work, which ran parallel to that of the Priestly Writing, and yet of avoiding the conclusion of the Yahwistic account foreshadowed in Gen. xii. 1–3 and of presenting, in fact, a quite different conclusion. In view of its sovereign handling of old traditions it would not have proved difficult for the Priestly Writing to avoid all reference to the idea of covenant if it had wanted to. The opposite seems to have been the case. By means of the covenants, i.e., the points in the Priestly Writing at which it was possible to fill out the narrative for once, a change from scanty genealogical connecting-links, chronological references etc., the Priestly Writer was able to present a view of the course of man's history and the early history of Israel which was formally in harmony with older traditions and yet came to a different conclusion. The fact that historical reality was all too frequently inadequately expressed would not have greatly troubled the Priestly Writer in view of his concern for themes rather than details. For instance, the connection of the Sabbath-day, the importance of which for the post-exilic community needs no emphasizing, with the creation of the world can have meant only one thing, namely that an ordinance applicable to all mankind was properly and adequately fulfilled only in Israel. The position is similar in the case of the prohibition to eat blood in connection with the covenant with Noah. As it stands the prohibition applies to all mankind, which starts afresh with Noah; but it is only fulfilled in the cultic community of Israel. Moreover, the fact that the idea of a covenant was no longer used to describe the events on Sinai which led to the establishment of the cultic community—assuming that the after-effects of Abraham's covenant in Gen. xvii could not still have been significant— may be an indication that the account of the Priestly Writing came to an end with the events that took place on the mount of God. In view of the oustanding importance of Israel, apparent in the above exposition, no further special covenant-making was necessary, because it was no longer necessary to take a further, substantially different course of history beyond Israel into account; but up to this point the covenant seems to have furnished the appropriate model for characterizing clearly and briefly the course of man's history terminating in Israel. Israel, in the shape of the cultic community characterized by the term 'edah, is the goal of God's ways with men in the eyes of the Priestly Writing. There is no denying that the thematic arrangement of the Yahwist's narrative work, according to which Israel had to regard itself as a bridge, so to speak, from the once universal, now destroyed and scattered, mankind to a new universal mankind, the contours of which are briefly sketched in Gen. xii. 1f., is not only not forgotten but quite deliberately corrected. This radical transformation, it may be assumed, was one of the most important impulses that led to the composition of the Priestly Writing. The Priestly Writing also was concerned with the granting of 'the most personal presence' of God, as Elliger[9] once put it; but the recipient of this gift of grace is exclusively Israel, as understood by the Priestly Writing, without recourse to other nations and their inclusion being felt to be of prime consideration. Without going into the numerous questions posed us by the Priestly Writing, there is one observation that is important in the context of the present study, namely that the Priestly Writing is dealing with the religious and cultic self-determination of Israel, whereas the relationship of the cultic community to the rest of the world—in other words, the eschatological view-point—is not regarded as equally important. For only where there has been steady, unclouded regard for the importance of Israel in relation to other nations is an eschatological perspective ever visible from time to time. But the question, in what circles and under what presuppositions such an understanding of Israel as is represented by the Priestly Writing developed, cannot be evaded altogether. There is no lack of lines which point to the past, such as, for instance, the fundamental deuteronomic demand for Israel's undivided love of the one God at the one cult-place, which is also taken for granted by the Priestly Writing. But this central demand of Deuteronomy need not necessarily issue in the Priestly Writer's view of Israel. It is true that the deuteronomic history deliberately avoided the question of the future form of Israel, but the influence of the deuteronomic-deuteronomistic preaching among those who remained in Palestine should not be underestimated.[10] For the appeal

[9] K. Elliger, 'Sinn und Ursprung der priesterschriftlichen Geschichtserzählung', *ZThK* 49 (1952), p. 127.
[10] E. Janssen, *Juda in der Exilszeit* (Diss. Kiel, 1956), esp. pp. 73f., has rightly pointed to this, even if he has limited the influences emanating from the exilic community in Babylon rather drastically; at any rate, the final form of post-exilic Israel was influenced by forces which are not to be sought in Palestine in the first place.

to obey the law (Deuteronomy) undoubtedly contributed towards keeping alive the hope that existing circumstances would be changed, and understandably change was, at first at any rate, thought of in terms of restoration. It is not easy to assess to what extent a message like that of Deutero-Isaiah exercised an invigorating influence on those who remained in Palestine. But in those circles which were familiar with exhortatory preaching in the manner of the deuterono-mistic speeches or the sermon-like addresses of the Book of Jeremiah a message of hope in the style of Deutero-Isaiah would not have been without influence, even though its effects may not have been visible until the early post-exilic period. For however we judge events in the quarter of a century between the Edict of Cyrus and the completion of the Temple under Darius I (515) the intention to build the Temple was forwarded considerably by the prophetic interpretation of contemporary events on the lips of Haggai and Zechariah, i.e. by an interpretation which may be regarded as pre-serving the old order but at the same time as eschatological. Even the history of the Chronicler, averse to every political adventure and absolutely rooted in the 'church views' of the Priestly Writing, could hardly ignore the assistance given by Haggai and Zechariah in the building of the Temple, although, it seems to me, the real effect of their work is not appreciated (Ezra v. 1; vi. 14). The Babylonian Diaspora was also passionately interested in the rebuilding of the Temple, but not in the sense of Haggai and Zechariah, who made the coming of salvation dependent on the erection of the Temple; rather, being acquainted with the theology and ecclesiology (*Verfas-sungsprogramm*) of Ezekiel at first hand, it was concerned to make the new Temple the cultic centre which would make possible a prosper-ous consolidation of relations in Palestine, combining loyalty to Persian rule with loyalty to the faith which had been handed down and which was the basis of Israel's special position. It was concerned to find a middle course between exaggerated expectations, doubtless encouraged by political disorders in the Persian Empire when Darius I came to power, and indifference bordering on apathy in the decades following the rebuilding of the Temple, which the appendages to the Book of Isaiah ('Trito-Isaiah') and the Book of Malachi are never tired of combating; such a path would exclude any political chauvin-ism and its associated dangers and at the same time prevent Israel's unique importance being swallowed up in religious apathy and indifference. This seems to have been the task with which those exiles in Babylon who were probably responsible for the Priestly Writing saw themselves confronted. They were aware of their importance, which had indeed been acknowledged in the past by prophetic voices (Jer. xxiv; Ezek. xi. 14f), and although Jeremiah had once warned the deported exiles (597) against rash action (Jer. xxix) they now regarded it as their duty to give public expression to their responsibility towards the situation in the homeland. Thus, paradoxical as it may seem, the religious forces which they had to try to regulate were the religious traditions of ancient Israel, which were by no means yet dead; misunderstanding of these traditions could have given rise to groundless hopes and further complications as well as disappointment and indifference; moreover, not least among such forces was the movement stemming from Deuteronomy, which with its demand for obedience to the Deuteronomic law constantly had the picture of early Israel before it. The circles responsible for the Priestly Writing may have agreed with Deuteronomy at critical points, e.g. in its fundamental demand for one cult-place or in its judgement of the Mosaic period as the classical period, in which the significance of Israel was first revealed, a time, therefore, which was permanently unique, but there is no doubt about the view of the Priestly Writing when it concerns the understanding of Israel's position, namely whether it was a religious people exposed to political decline or a religious community raised above the rest of mankind by cult and law, a church. Whatever we decide about the 'inner' history of what we are accustomed to designate by the symbol P, whether, in view of the repetitions and discrepancies within the narrative of the Priestly Writing, we should reckon with secondary additions or with a combination of two parallel recensions, and whatever we decide about the way the different materials within the legal sections were combined in the written version and publication of what we call the Priestly Codex, there is visible a well thought out plan, which can only be explained in terms of the historical situation in the first century of Persian rule. There may be some dispute over the exact contents of the law-book of Moses that was given to Ezra, priest and scribe of the God of heaven, to fulfil his mission; opinions also differ as to whether it is more illuminating to understand the work of Ezra as prior to that of Nehemiah or vice versa—the traditional view that Ezra came first and strove for a constitutional-religious reformation of public life and then, because of certain difficulties, especially in the vexed question of mixed marriages, steps were taken towards political independence insofar as Persian provincial administration allowed, still seems to me to offer a more satisfactory explanation of the historical development than the reverse assumption, although in recent years this has been advocated with increasing force; but there should be no doubt that the formation of the post-exilic community is connected with the traditions which found literary expression in the Priestly Writing; hardly any modern scholar seriously disputes this. Ezra's code, then, embodies the Law in the sense that it continues the ancient sacral law, which may be regarded as the essential part of the Priestly Writing—essential in that it made it possible to carry through the distinction and isolation of Israel as a holy community. Unlike the Elohistic account, for instance, into which the Book of the Covenant, now interpreted as part of the ancient sacral law as a result of the Decalogue, has been inserted, although it was clearly felt to be a heterogeneous block of material, the narrative of the Priestly Writing, which already in the account of creation had understood separation and division as the principle of creation, is simply the path of world-history, by which man arrives—through the doors of separate covenants—at the central point of creation, the holy community established on the mount of God, in whose midst God's gracious presence has become reality through his revelation to Moses. It would not be true to say that the narrative of the Priestly Writing is not equal to this task of bridging the time span from the origin of the world to the time of Moses in a few grandiose chapters, although the unusual combination of genealogical references, numbers and lists with divine oracles of revelation does not always make for vivid narrative. But vividness should not be expected when description is subordinate to the need to give a brief, clear definition of what Israel has to stand for. Thus in the midst of the abundant variety of sacred traditions in the rest of the Pentateuch the account of the Priestly Writing seems rather like an extensive aetiology, seeking to demonstrate with summary facts the historical path by which the community of Israel in Moses' day came into being.

It might, of course, be objected that such a view would favour an eschatological expectation, because the restoration of Israel in the sense of 'edah yisrael, which was being necessitated by historical changes, could hardly be understood apart from an eschatological viewpoint. But the Priestly Writing, which ended with the Israel of Moses' day, clearly had no intention of attributing any fundamental importance to the further historical growth of Israel. Hence the historical field is limited from the start to the period from the beginning of the world to the formation of the 'edah yisrael, without any real expectation that what came into being at that time would undergo further development. In spite of its historical introduction, therefore, the narrative of the Priestly Writing is ultimately the expression of an unhistorical approach. The history of a people of God may, of course, be pursued and described in full detail; but it only gains its distinctive interest from the attempt to portray the relation of this people of God to the rest of mankind. The history of a religious community, a church in the sense of *'edah yisrael*, can only have meaning as a history of antecedents (*Vorgeschichte*), in that it describes how the creation and divine position of this unusual community, to which there is no longer—nor ever shall be—any parallel in the sphere of history and the secular world, came about. What may still be called history after the formation of such a community is at best an esoteric history, played out between the divine author and his divine creation. Obviously, the Priestly Writing is concerned amongst other things to portray in a historical introduction how this community of Israel came into being, so that it may then exempt Israel from the influence of historical relationships on the ground that it is unique.

That the redactor of the Priestly Writing would link it with the other narratives of the later Pentateuch could hardly have been anticipated by the original authors; but such a step may be justified as an interpretation of ancient traditions, because the understanding of Israel proposed by the Priestly Writing probably established itself fairly quickly and extensively. We shall fall back, therefore, once more on the work of Rost cited above, turning our attention, however, to an area which Rost only touches on incidentally—namely, the fact that outside the Priestly Writing, particularly in certain Psalms, ideas which are in line with the Priestly Writing's understanding of Israel, but which would not have been adequately expressed by *'am* or *ḳahal*, are linked with the term *'edah*. When, for instance, in the Psalms the *'edah* of the righteous (Ps. i. 5) is contrasted with the *'edah* of evil doers (Ps. xxii. 17) or the *'edah* of ruthless men (Ps. lxxxvi. 14; cf. also Job xv. 34), the term used to describe the various shades of opinion within the post-exilic community is one which refers in the first place to a religio-cultic viewpoint and is governed by the understanding which the Jewish community of this period as a whole had of itself. But this conventicle-type distinction was only taken up after such predominantly religious criteria had become prevalent and determinative. Even the society of the foreign, hostile world is described by the term *'edah* on one occasion (Ps. lxviii.31), not only because it is being criticized by the use of *'edah*, but because a confrontation between human groups or associations and Yahweh, irrespective of the nature of these groups, immediately awakens the same understanding of a divine-human relationship as that contained pre-eminently in the term '*edah*. The fact that other terms are also used (e.g. Ps. cxi. 11—*sod y*^e*sarim*) should not be overlooked; but they are synonyms which share in the same range of meaning as is associated primarily with '*edah*.[11]

We turn now to a brief consideration of the work of the Chronicler, comprising the two Books of Chronicles and the Books of Ezra and Nehemiah; once again we shall be concerned simply with the view of Israel governing this account, which stretches from the time of David to the end of the activity of Ezra and Nehemiah. In his monograph on the view of history in the work of the Chronicler von Rad[12] has devoted a section to the term 'Israel' in the Books of Ezra and Nehemiah and in the Books of Chronicles; he comes to the conclusion that the fact of the substantially reduced area of Israel is taken into account, but that the significant term Israel is preferred for the surviving tribes of Judah and Benjamin (pp. 24f.), inasmuch as in the Books of Chronicles the criterion is the relation to the Davidic covenant, so that—even if it is not always consistently maintained— in the period after the division of the kingdom the name Israel can only properly be used for the parts which still belong to the house of David. It may be noticed in passing that a similar procedure can be observed in the first Book of Maccabees, where the name Israel is used for what is only a part of the whole, although here—at a later date and under different circumstances—the interests of Israel are unhesitatingly identified with the concerns of the Maccabean party (1 Macc. vii. 21; ix. 27, 73). In addition von Rad has also demonstrated (p. 8; 18 etc.) that the terminology and certain theological expressions in the work of the Chronicler are to be connected with the tradition of Deuteronomy rather than that of the

---

[11] The reason why the Greek equivalent for '*edah*, namely *sunagoge* (cf. Rost, pp. 122f.), is not used by Josephus to describe various groups and sects (he always uses the term *hairesis* instead) is undoubtedly connected with the fact that at a later period *sunagoge* denoted an assembly room. Rost (pp. 134f.) has given a good explanation for the juxtaposition of *ekklesia* (= *ḳahal*) and *sunagoge* in 1 Macc. The political aim of the Maccabees, which became obvious at a later stage of the struggle, namely the formation of an independent Jewish state, made the term *ekklesia* preferable, especially when it concerned the levy for war (cf. 1 Macc. iii. 13), whereas the 'Pious', regarded as a cultic association, were termed a *sunagoge* (1 Macc. ii. 42); similarly the 'Community of the New Covenant at Damascus' was always called an '*edah*.

[12] G. von Rad, *Das Geschichtsbild des chronistischen Werkes*, BWANT IV/3 (1930), pp. 19f., 25f.

Priestly Writing, which is chronologically closer.[13] This affinity
with the deuteronomic-deuteronomistic viewpoint is also influenced
by the fact that the Chronicler is dealing with the same period that
occupies the centre of the deuteronomic history and consequently is
largely constructed on the deuteronomic model. But this makes it
difficult to understand why the Chronicler makes his account begin
with the Davidic period after his genealogical preface; his deuterono-
mistic model could equally well have served as a source for the period
from Moses to David. But he obviously had no interest in the pre-
monarchic period of Israel. It should be borne in mind, as Rudolph
suggested long ago and recently emphasized again,[14] that 'the
Chronicler seeks to portray the realization of theocracy on the soil
of Israel', in the way it had eventually taken shape in the election
of Judah and Jerusalem. The emphasis had become necessary in
view of the different interpretation of the Samaritans. This is the
reason for the special interest of the Chronicler in the Davidic
covenant and also for his efforts to give David a share in the building
of the Temple, which was completed by his successor, by attributing
to him careful advance plans. After the dissolution of the monarchy
the Temple in Jerusalem which was so closely connected with the
Judaean king was the last link connecting the community of the
Chronicler with the Jerusalem of the monarchical period; hence it
possessed a special importance as a symbol of historical continuity.
Hence the political event of the division of the kingdom after the
death of Solomon was also given the character of a schism in the view
of the Chronicler, and the history of the divided kingdoms, enclosed
by the two appeals to return made by the Judaean kings Abijah
(2 Chron. xiii. 4–12) and Hezekiah (2 Chron. xxx. 6–9), is obviously
meant to be understood in such a way that only the part which
remained loyal to the Davidic covenant is to be regarded as the true
Israel. For 'the Chronicler took up the principle of the sole legitimacy
of the Jerusalem Temple proposed by the Deuteronomist and linked
it with the promise to the House of David; it was, therefore, clear
that after the "division of the kingdom" in Israel there could only be
apostatizers.'[15] Moreover, the common possession of the Pentateuch
makes it clear that there was little or no difference between the Jews
and the Samaritans in their estimate of the early history of Israel.[16]
It must, therefore, have been all the more galling for the Samaritans

[13] Cf. also W. Rudolph, *Chronikbücher*, HAT I no. 21 (1955), pp. xivf.
[14] Rudolph, *Chronikbücher*, p. viiif.
[15] K. Galling, *Die Bücher der Chronik, Esra, Nehemia*, ATD 12 (1954), p. 15.
[16] Cf. M. Noth, *Überlieferungsgeschichtliche Studien*, I, p. 175.

that the Chronicler reckoned with a new covenant, namely, the covenant with David, after the Sinaitic covenant, which was the conclusion of the history of Israel described by the Pentateuch (under the influence of the Priestly Writing); the kernel of this new covenant was the election of Judah and Jerusalem, and the Chronicler was understandably only too ready to utilize the deuteronomistic model. This reference back to the deuteronomistic work of history, however, although welcome to the Chronicler, does not prevent him presupposing the Priestly Writing's view of Israel, and despite the absence of the term *'edah*, which Rudolph (p. xv) rightly points out, he describes the period of history which interests him as if Israel in the time of David was a religious community in the same way that it was in his own day.[17] The Priestly Writing ended its account with the Israel of Moses' day, and in the cult-community on Sinai introduced the Israel which was again to achieve reality in the re-establishment of the post-exilic community under Ezra and Nehemiah, without being compelled, however, to depict the continuity of the two communities in detail; but the Chronicler, in view of the controversy with the Samaritans, felt he could not avoid this task. Hence he took the story further in the manner of the Priestly Writing to the point where the community then existing in his day had been freshly constituted. This context alone explains one striking observation which is particularly important for what follows.

We are indebted to Rudolph for the valuable indication that 'the view of the Chronicler is fundamentally different from the main O.T. line, the prophetic view, through the almost complete disappearance of eschatological expectation'. He explains this by saying 'that the actual Jewish community, such as we read about in Neh. xii. 44–xiii. 3 particularly, embodied the theocratic ideal to such an extent that there was no longer any need for eschatological expectation'.[18] Rudolph elaborates this difference 'from the real O.T. view of God's rule' by noting another essential difference, namely the lack of interest shown by the Chronicler in the religious fate of the Gentile nations . . .; he is too occupied with the debate with false brethren, the Samaritans.'[19] There is clearly some connection between these two points of differentiation. For it is only where the fate of the Gentile world is not dismissed as of no concern that the question of the future relationship of the theocracy to the Gentile world arises

---

[17] Cf. O. Eissfeldt, *The Old Testament: An Introduction*, p. 539.
[18] Rudolph, *Chronikbücher*, p. xxiii.
[19] Rudolph, *Chronikbücher*, p. xxiv.

and opens the eyes to eschatological expectation, just as, *vice versa*, an eschatological viewpoint cannot disregard the question of the future destiny of the Gentiles. Rudolph's argument that the Chronicler was so convinced of the embodiment of his theocratic ideal within the Jewish community that there was no longer any need of eschatological expectation is undoubtedly correct; it must be added, however, that the conviction was not primarily his own creation but was taken over by him from the Priestly Writing's understanding of how Israel ought to regard itself. One of the marks of the Priestly Writing's view of history in our opinion was the plan of tracing the course of world history, punctuated by the great covenant-ceremonies, only as far as the establishment of the cultic community on Mount Sinai, which marked the culmination of God's dealings with his creation and after which there was no prospect of any fundamental change; hence the statements contained in the Pentateuch are quite sufficient to enable Israel to understand itself. Here are the seeds of what may be called a non-eschatological view of history in the Old Testament. But in order to exonerate the Priestly Writing of any possible charge of narrow-minded shortsightedness it should be pointed out that, in view of the desperate situation in Palestine in the half-century following the rebuilding of the Temple, and in view of the oscillation between apathy (cf. Malachi) and glowing expectations (cf. Isa. lvi–lxvi), the Priestly Writing considered itself compelled to take this rigorous step, if it was to establish a foundation that would guarantee some degree of permanence for a settled Israel. This step of creating a link across the centuries with the Israelite community of the Sinaitic period may be called unhistorical; but Deuteronomy had done the same, by making the Israel of Josiah's time be instructed by Moses and thus by tracing it back into the situation of the Mosaic period. But the fact that the Chronicler expressly confirmed his non-eschatological view of history when the Jewish community based on the Priestly Writing's views had been in existence longer, and this at a time when, as in previous decades, eschatological expectation within the community was by no means silent but had been given new life by the various additions and expansions to the prophetic writings—we shall come back to this later—compels the impression that the Chronicler's work of history is influenced not only by an outward looking anti-Samaritan aim, but also by an inward looking anti-eschatological point of view. As a result of the situation indicated by the Samaritan controversy, the Chronicler obviously had no room for the hopes of restoration and expectations of reunification that were still probably very much alive due to the message of the former prophets. It seems plausible, therefore, to see the polemical side of the Chronicler's work not only in the rejection of the Samaritan heresy, however important this was for the Chronicler, but also in the refusal to entertain eschatological expectations of any sort, however conceived, which still lived on in the Jerusalem community of that period. This, however, presupposes a rather longer period between the establishment of the post-exilic community under Ezra/Nehemiah and the composition of the Chronicler's work. We must, therefore, touch on this question also, even if only briefly.

Attempts have been made to connect the origin of the Chronicler's work of history with the Samaritan schism, although the precise date of this cannot be fixed with any certainty. The suggestion that the Samaritan schism presupposes the background of political change which followed the transfer of Persian rule to the Macedonian victors under Alexander is extremely attractive.[20] But there is certainly no possibility of definite proof and one must allow a certain latitude of date in both directions. Thus, Galling suggests the last two decades of the Persian Empire, but dates the conclusion of the Chronicler's work, together with the extensive additions which he ascribes to a second Chronicler, about one hundred years later.[21] In the present study, on the basis of the analysis of eschatological passages from the prophetic books in the next chapter, we have attempted to date the work of the Chronicler after the Samaritan schism, and, therefore— if this division is to be connected with the events of Alexander's expedition—in the decades after 330 B.C. At any rate, the date suggested by Rudolph—about 400 B.C. or a few years later[22]—seems to me to founder on the shortness of the interval which he posits between the establishment of the community under Nehemiah/Ezra and the composition of the Chronicler's work. Recourse to the Maccabean period, an expedient sometimes invoked in a previous generation,[23] can hardly be right.

At any rate, one has to proceed from the assumption that the Chronicler was indifferent, if not hostile, to an eschatological expectation which must still have had a formative influence on the life of the community of his day. This is certainly not due to a desire on

---

[20] Noth, *Überlieferungsgeschichtliche Studien* I, pp. 154f., 164f.; *The History of Israel*, p. 355.

[21] Galling, *Die Bücher der Chronik*, ATD 12 (1954), pp. 14f.

[22] Rudolph, *Chronikbücher*, p. x; cf. also his commentary on Ezra and Nehemiah, HAT 1 no. 20, p. xxivf.

[23] Details in Rudolph, *Chronikbücher*, p. x.

D

his part to minimize the great significance of the prophets; the Chronicler's description of the monarchical period contains frequent reference to the considerable influence of the prophetic word. But he prefers to regard prophecy in a manner which could almost be called purely historical. In this form prophecy performed a valuable guardian rôle until the community based on the Law of Moses received its final shape. The kings, priests and prophets, who strove for the erection of the Temple, true cult and proper obedience, and who represent the three great offices of Israel at the time of the monarchy, made a valuable contribution to the constitution of the new community and were thus concerned to ensure the continuity of this community with the Israel of the Mosaic period. Now, however, what they contributed has been taken up in the theocracy which now represents Israel. That this view of the Chronicler made converts is proved by a reference in Josephus; his statements must be treated with caution, but in this case they are probably based on unimpeachable and reliable traditions. In the final section of his description of the rule of Johannes Hyrcanus[24] Josephus mentions that God's favour towards the Hasmonaeans has permitted the union of the three highest positions, which we may understand as *charismata*, namely the government of his people, the office of High Priest and the gift of prophecy. The Hasmonaean possesses the *munus triplex*! This view corresponds exactly to that which the Chronicler holds of his community as a whole, namely that the old charismatic gifts have found their permanent home and are, therefore, to be considered illegitimate outside this community.

The interpretation of the Chronicler is also responsible for the arbitrary abbreviation of the seventy-year period, which according to the well-known passages of the Book of Jeremiah (xxv. 11f.; xxix. 10) ought to denote the period of the exile or the destruction of Jerusalem. Even if this number probably represents a *vaticinium ex eventu*, the reference of the Book of Zechariah (i. 12) to these seventy years in the context of tense expectations which had a decisive effect on the re-erection of the Temple shows that this number is primarily meant to describe the period from the destruction of the Temple to its restoration (587/6–515 B.C.). The Chronicler also makes use of this number (2 Chron. xxxvi. 21); but by linking it with the edict of Cyrus, he makes it clear that on his view this decree of the king brings to an end the period encompassed by the seventy years, because the first steps which ultimately led to the formation of the

[24] Cf. Jos. Ant. xiii. 10. 7 with Bell. i. 2. 8.

new Israel could now be taken; the completion of this restoration made eschatological hope pointless. On the other hand, the fresh interpretation of these seventy years, granted to Daniel when he was living in exile (Dan. ix), can only be understood as a protest of re-awakened eschatological conviction, which in its interpretation of the former prophets wishes to emphasize the eschatological significance of certain revelations of these prophets. This protest of the apocalyptist is directed against the then prevalent view of the priestly aristocracy at Jerusalem, whose understanding of Israel was deeply influenced by the work of the Chronicler, an understanding, it should be noted, that very soon after the beginning of the insurrection was also adopted by the Maccabean movement and that subsequently led to differences within the anti-Hellenistic opposition. It must, of course, be admitted that such a resurgence of eschatological interpretation of historical events as is to be found in the Book of Daniel was closely connected with the political events at the time of Antiochus IV Epiphanes, especially since there had been no lack of disturbances in Palestine following the change of rule from the Ptolemies to the Seleucids.[25] But the influences at work from the political side were only the outward occasions for the manifestation of eschatological expectations, which, although hidden beneath the surface, had never completely died out. These expectations had, however, undergone a change of form, apparently as a direct result of that other great change which Israel had in the meantime experienced, namely, when the people of God became an ecclesiastical community. This sociological and structural change meant no more and no less than the end of the prophetic, i.e., historical, eschatology; it was now superfluous. For the change that had taken place in the Jerusalem community, the transformation of the nation into a community resembling a church, a change which made it possible to remedy defects and expunge errors, although it also meant that the structure of the new community was no longer subject to the variations of historical change, made men realize that the prophetic eschatology, which had the nation at its centre, could no longer be maintained in the traditional sense; it had lost its point. The goal of earlier eschatological expectation, the winding-up of the nation on the lines of the plan of Yahweh proclaimed by the prophets, was in principle already attained in a community founded exclusively on

<hr>

[25] This has been rightly emphasized by Rowley, who cites several examples from the early history of prophecy; cf. H. H. Rowley, *The Relevance of Apocalyptic* (1963[3]), pp. 16ff.

cult and law; the only justification for the maintenance of eschatological hopes was that they confirmed what was, in fact, already the case. It was possible for plans of reform to be pursued in such a community and it was quite possible for a situation to occur in which a reformation seemed necessary, and this would produce either the desired result or schism. Such an attempt had obviously been planned by the Hellenistic reform party under Antiochus IV, with the perfidious intent of gradually dismantling the distinctive life of Israel, which was based on ancestral faith and practice, in order that they might live as Greeks among Greeks. A restoration focused on the earlier *nation* of Israel, and directed by the eschatological expectations which took shape at a time when Israel still existed as a nation, no longer appeared worth striving after. This indifference to eschatology among the priestly aristocracy at Jerusalem had serious consequences, it should be noted. A certain emptiness or aimlessness must have been noticeable, since there was no expectation of anything further that could have imported new vitality to the religious life. Hence, the circles of the higher priesthood were prone to follow any attractive possibility from outside that entered their range of vision. It is not surprising, therefore, that attempts at Hellenization in the first decades of Seleucid rule fell on fertile ground in Jerusalem. The gradual decline of eschatological expectation, which was regarded as superseded rather than crushed, undoubtedly made a substantial contribution to the secularization of certain influential groups within the priesthood.

But hope, waiting on God, is an integral part of faith, and when faith is limited to the purely cultic sphere, without a vital relationship to historical events, it cannot find full expression. Israel was only able to express its deepest religious experiences when it found itself *in statu promissionis*. Whatever decision is reached about the origins of eschatology in the Old Testament, eschatological expectations in the decades which concern us here were firmly linked with the message of the earlier prophets, in which the historical process, the fulfilment of Yahweh's plan in the sphere of history, played a special rôle. It should be borne in mind, of course, that at that time prophecy was regarded retrospectively in a generalized, oversimplified way. The old contrasts between prophecies of salvation and judgement, for instance, were obviously no longer felt with the same sharpness. We must also take into account the fact that the secondary additions to the writings of the prophets also contain elements from the earlier salvation prophecy; such verses may now seem out of place on the lips of former opposition-prophets, but they were regarded as corroboration of the comparatively rare salvation prophecies of the old and venerable prophets of judgement.

A tendency towards generalization always thrives on the idea that a historical event or movement of the past can be treated as a self-contained entity. To that extent the attitude of the Chronicler to prophecy is quite natural. But as a component part of the message of Yahweh's spokesmen, the prophets, eschatological hope once possessed the same honour as was attributed to the word of Yahweh. Just as the revelation of Yahweh recorded in the Torah had obtained canonical validity, so the prophetic word of Yahweh, including its eschatology, pressed towards validity in the present. The interpretative clauses which had been added, particularly in the sphere of prophetic eschatology, laid claim to be regarded as no less legitimate than the interpretative *toroth* which had been added to the older legal corpora; the later origin of these *toroth* was certainly not in any doubt, even if they only gained acceptance because of the key-phrase, 'Law of Moses'. The view that was sometimes put forward by scribes of a Pharisaic outlook at a later date, namely that the prophets are to be regarded as exponents and interpreters of the *Torah*—not without justice, bearing in mind the way the prophets take up the ancient sacral law—should also be understood from the standpoint that here, in a similar manner to the canonization of the *Torah* (Law) and not unrelated to it, a further step was being taken towards the canonization of ancient traditions, even though it was not undertaken by the same official circles of the Jerusalem community. In other words, although officially within the Jewish community adequate place was no longer given to the real importance of the prophetic word in its primary eschatological sense, there were circles which were still convinced of the contemporary validity of the prophetic word; it is understandable that these circles should have felt it necessary to band together in a conventicle type of association on the lines of the community at Jerusalem with which they were familiar. Such an 'internal' separation need not have led to outward division as long as no particular occasion arose. But if, as a result of the non-eschatological and increasingly aimless attitude of the leading priestly aristocracy, we should take into account a tendency to give way to foreign influences, especially Hellenistic, then it is understandable that the circles of this secret isolationism received fresh encouragement because on their view the model of the true Israel was more fully embodied in their own ranks.

At this point the first consequence of the change in structure which Israel had undergone makes itself manifest. Within a national body, even if it was theologically regarded as God's people, opposition movements could be formed and tolerated without endangering the unity of the nation; we think, for instance, of the Nazarenes, the Rechabites, and of certain opposition forces within prophecy, movements which embodied in various ways the old charismatic past within a dynastic, institutional Israel. Within a religious community, i.e., one based primarily on cult and law, an opposition movement assumed a more rigid cast, however. Not only was it possible for it to be considered as more than a reaction against a dominant line, but it lodged its own claims to orthodoxy and exclusiveness, for it, too, depended on the principle of community; at all events, the tendency for it to become a new independent community alongside, and to some extent replacing, the previous body, could not be avoided permanently. Such a divergence could not have taken place overnight, in view of the numerous points (law, cult) they had in common, holding the divergent groups together. In short, we shall have to think in terms of a longer period— from the foundation of the new community under Ezra/Nehemiah up to the religious conflict under Antiochus IV Epiphanes, during which the emphasis undoubtedly falls on the last hundred years, when these contrasts which are hidden beneath the surface must have been taking shape, until a specific occasion brought them into the open. In retrospect it may be regarded as significant that it took a long time before an occasion for division presented itself, because outward calm usually sharpens existing hidden differences rather than solves them, and other differences, which were at first quite peripheral, can add their weight to the existing problems. If, then, the various attitudes to the eschatological question may be regarded as the decisive point of difference, then it is easy to see how the cleavage which is visible at this point was bound to lead either to greater indifference or to a sharper definition of the eschatological point of view. This stricter definition has obviously found expression in the conversion of the prophetic eschatology to the apocalyptic view of the future.

That acquaintance with foreign religious views of pre-eminently eschatological content played an important rôle in this process has long been suspected and there is no need to set out the reasons at great length here. In his researches into the origins of Judaism, E. Meyer gave a great deal of room to the possibility of religious ideas from Iran having influenced the Jewish community.[26] We should not, of course, overlook the difficulty that in this particular sphere, where religious ideas were not unimportant, there is to be observed a striking openness to certain convictions of foreign extraction; this is in contrast to the otherwise obvious resistance of the Jewish community to everything foreign. Since we are concerned primarily with eschatological ideas in this matter of foreign influence, we are reluctant to assume such an openness to foreign ideas in circles that were sceptical or antagonistic towards an eschatological point of view. It might be suggested, however, that in the first decades of Persian rule, when there were still lively attempts at restoration, a very positive influence of foreign ideas, in this case Iranian, could have given a new impulse to native convictions and could also have been regarded as an enrichment of the world of received belief. But it is most improbable that this influence could already have been in full spate, because the influence of the various prophetic traditions was still very strong, although elements of these traditions had undergone a certain measure of development (a more transcendental view of God, the rise of angelology etc.). It is certainly far from easy to contemplate the official Jewish community being influenced by foreign ideas, seeing that it had been formed with the express intention of intercepting and neutralizing possible eschatological attempts at restoration. There is, however, a great deal to be said for the view that it was in the long interval between 400 B.C. and 200 B.C. that the later apocalyptic view began to establish itself on a large scale. This must be connected with the attempts to actualize and maintain the eschatology which had been officially relegated to the periphery. A religious movement which occupies the periphery is usually glad to deck itself out with new elements in order to make itself more attractive and to attain greater recognition. Such a superficial explanation, however, is certainly inadequate. The circles which were receptive to these new ideas probably recognized in apocalyptic, i.e., cosmic-dualistic, views simply the keener, fresher and more pregnant expression of what prophetic eschatology also sought to depict. It is understandable, therefore, that at first previous expectations on accepted strategic points were emphasized by specific features of the new world of ideas, but that, in view of the unsympathetic attitude of the official community, more and more borrowing

---

[26] E. Meyer, *Die Entstehung des Judentums* (1896)—*Ursprung und Anfänge des Christentums* II (1921), pp. 41–57; 95–120; cf. also his *Geschichte des Altertums* IV 1, ed. by E. Stier (1944⁴), pp. 157–218.

became necessary because men recognized their own situation more pertinently in this dualistic outlook and were, therefore, ready to accept foreign ideas on a large scale. The distinctiveness of the situation, however, was determined by the fact that they belonged to a community which they felt was of unique significance and stood out from the rest of the world but from which they felt divorced in view of the way this community was developing; hence they made use of foreign dualistic expressions to clarify this distinction which they felt was so important. Thus, in a community which by its religious structure was separate from the rest of the world and which was opposed to every external influence, these eschatologically minded groups seem to have been the weak spot, through which foreign ideas might find a way in. But since these groups also depended on the same principle of community that characterized the wider community, they began to strengthen their position gradually by secluding themselves in conventicles without separating officially from the wider community, whose temple-cult and law they still adhered to; in fact, perhaps to strengthen their own position they became more zealous in their pursuit of the Law and its cult. In addition, they maintained an eschatological view in obedience to the prophetic word; it was given a fresh interpretation, however, with the help of foreign, dualistic ideas and this intensified their opposition to the official community. There was no reason or pretext for the representatives of the theocracy to oppose this new development, especially since it is not impossible that there was a growing conviction amongst the ruling classes also that something in Israel's religious outlook which had once been given expression through the message of the prophets was now missing or neglected. Thus, the eschatological conventicle paved the way for the understandable but fatal attempt to translate the dualistic world-view into the terms of their own situation, which was marked by opposition to the official community, and thus to convert cosmic dualism into an ecclesiastical and confessional dualism. This development must have been brewing for a long time beneath the surface; but it needed only the slightest provocation for the latent tension to reveal itself. Evidence of this is provided at the end of this still open period of development by the Book of Daniel, which is to be attributed to the eschatological conventicles. In Dan. xii, which agrees with certain statements in 2 Macc. (cf. ch. vii for instance) in the matter of personal resurrection, the world outside Israel is categorically excluded; the resurrection applies only to Israel. This undoubtedly expresses the doctrinal unanimity which existed with regard to Israel's unique position amongst the nations of the world, a view maintained both by the official community and by the eschatological groups. At the same time the hitherto concealed opposition stands out plainly, for the paradox of a double recurrence entails that that section of Israel which was indifferent to eschatology will experience the truth and accuracy of eschatological faith—in the form of punishment, insofar as it will be for them a resurrection 'to eternal shame'; the downfall of what represents Israel in the world is more painful and terrible for the section of Israel which is indifferent to eschatology than the fate of the Gentile world, which is excluded from the resurrection. One might, in fact, say that this represents the final confirmation of that separation within Israel referred to by Isaiah when he spoke of days such as had not been seen since the secession of Ephraim from Judah coming upon King Ahaz and his people as a result of the king's decision regarding Immanuel (Isa. vii. 17); the prophet was obviously contemplating a new division, more serious and far-reaching in its consequences than the schism which followed Solomon's death. The eschatological groups, which depended on the interpretation of the prophetic word to give them life, did not think it erroneous to expect that the Samaritan schism would be followed by a final and conclusive separation, from which the section of the people of God which according to Dan. xii would participate in the resurrection to life would emerge as the true Israel. But it should be remembered that the contrast which a passage like Dan. xii exhibits with utter clarity grew up gradually, and it has been blurred again by the use of traditional elements from the prophetic eschatology which had in view the consummation of the world. It is true that the apocalyptic-dualistic interpretation of the old eschatological ideas reveals the faith that did, in fact, activate such groups; but there have certainly been advantages as well as disadvantages in the fact that the two attitudes towards eschatology, although sometimes mutually exclusive, have been preserved in their hermeneutical relationship.

Thus, the transformation of the nation of Israel into the community of Yahweh established the basis which inevitably led to the change of the prophetic eschatology into the apocalyptic view of the future, as soon as the new community, itself possibly regarded as the fulfilment of an earlier cherished hope in connection *inter alia* with the remnant idea, was confronted with the claims of eschatological faith once again. Subject to all the limitations of a onesided point of view we could pointedly describe this change as follows. The old prophetic eschatology embodied the future hope of a nation which was conscious of being separate from the other nations of the world as a result of its relationship to God, although it did not overlook the significance of this for the other nations, pressing, in fact, towards a consummation of creation without surrendering its own privileges; apocalyptic eschatology, on the other hand, expressed the future hope of a community which was conscious of being a religious body absolutely separate from the national and religious life of the rest of mankind and which, being unique, could only express a future hope in terms of the manifestation of its own distinctive existence, while living at the same time in the belief that 'the manner of this world is passing away'. In the exilic and early post-exilic period hopes of restoration played a substantial part both positively and negatively in leading to the establishment of the new community in which these hopes were to find fulfilment; after the formation of the community a new emphasis on eschatological faith produced a fundamental alteration and change, because otherwise there was no hope of demonstrating the existence of a community basically different from the rest of creation. It is inadmissible, therefore, to regard the assumption of a dualistic world-view of Iranian origin as a capital error which exercised an unfortunate influence on the further history of Jewish religion; primarily, foreign ideas simply provided the material with which to recognize and describe the existing situation better.

It is in this direction that one must seek an explanation for the transformation of eschatological expectations, which without minimizing the importance of foreign influences is more firmly rooted in the sphere of Old Testament traditions. For the theologically momentous transition from the nation of Israel to the community of Yahweh, which may be regarded as an act of withdrawal into a specifically religious sphere, bears within itself the seed of sectarian narrowness, when one compares this with the very prominent position amongst the nations which Israel claimed for itself at an earlier date. This was the beginning of a path from which there could be no turning back in the case of possible theological differences within the community, a path that was bound to lead to further divisions and splits as a result of the claim to represent the true Israel. Because it was the differences in eschatology that led to this course of events it is easy to see why it was the deviations of these schismatic groups that were developed and elaborated, and because the groups responsible for this development were essentially independent and not subject to the regimentation of any official authority outside of their own ranks it is again easy to see why this elaboration and development in a free, unregimented form evoked a constant ferment and flux of new ideas. A sectarian spirit such as we may assume in these conventicles is in a position to imbibe new ideas, because it is basically concerned only with itself, and yet must be at pains to exaggerate nuances, to sever its ties not only with the official community but also with groups related by common tradition and to direct its gaze chiefly to the future. Thus the motley variety of apocalyptic writings in the later period is easy to understand against the background of a common origin differentiated by certain individual traits, because there was no regimenting, official hand in the initial stages and the interpretation of the old prophetic traditions was taken over by rampant speculation.

To what extent the origin of the synagogue and the shape of synagogue worship in the post-exilic period are to be connected with these eschatological groups is a difficult question which requires special consideration and cannot be gone into at this juncture. There should be no doubt, however, that the tremendous impact of the religious conflict under Antiochus IV Epiphanes together with the Maccabean rising and the vigorous fight for power by the Maccabean party contributed greatly to the process of further division. If it is correct to see in the Pharisees and Essenes—it is not accidental that these names are first mentioned in the work of Josephus in the second half of the second century B.C.—successors of the Hasidic groups in the period of religious conflict, groups which may in turn be derived from the eschatological groups investigated here, then the history of these groups illustrates the continuation of this divisive process. Such a view would take us too far into a later period; it would also necessitate a more detailed treatment of the groups which we have to assume behind the Dead Sea Scrolls, behind the Damascus document and behind the accounts of the Essenes in various parts of Josephus; the time does not seem ripe for this at present. However these groups are related to one another, it may safely be said that the motives for separation and a sectarian manner of life are to be sought in the impulse to realise in various ways the ideal picture of the true Israel, a process in which both the intensification of legal observance and special encouragement of eschatological expectations probably played an important rôle. Even if the Pharisees are to be contrasted fairly sharply with these groups insofar as they rejected a sectarian seclusion and made a determined attempt to secure spiritual authority over the people as a partisan movement—undoubtedly modelled on the partisan organization of the Maccabean movement—yet they share with these other fringe-groups of the Jewish community a common descent from the *Hasidim*. It may, perhaps, be objected that in the later Rabbinic theology there is a definite reserve towards the apocalyptic view of the future. But between the bellicose Pharisees who scuffled with the Hasmonaeans Johannes Hyrcanus and Alexander Jannaeus, and the Rabbis of A.D. 100 who were the undisputed spiritual rulers of the people, there is a fairly long period of development amounting to almost two hundred years, a period in which political events exercized a decisive rôle.[27] As regards the Rabbis of a later period the judgement of Volz may be correct[28]; but the fact that even in this late period a Rabbi of the standing of Ben-Akiba succumbed to the messianic-eschatological hopes of the Bar-Cochba rising may indicate that remembrance of the origins of the Pharisaic movement was not completely dead even at that time.

This study is concerned with an earlier period, which is far poorer in sources; due allowance may be made, therefore, for hypothetical suggestions which seek to illuminate these two dark centuries. Nevertheless, we cannot escape the obligation of verifying whether we can recognize traces of the change of form from the eschatology of an older period to apocalyptic, even if only in its initial stages. We may expect such traces mostly in passages of prophetic literature whose late origin is undisputed. We are thinking, for instance, of the 'Isaiah Apocalypse' (Isa. xxiv–xxvii), the additions to the Book of Zechariah ('Trito-Zechariah', Zech. xii–xiv) and the two final chapters of the Book of Joel; these are the selected independent units which we shall examine purely from the standpoint advanced above.

---

[27] Cf. E. Bickermann, *Die Makkabäer* (1938), pp. 59f. The account of L. Baeck, *Die Pharisäer* (1934) goes back more to a later period of Pharisaism, while R. T. Herford, *Judaism in the New Testament Period* (1928), makes too direct a connection between the prophets and the Pharisees (cf. for instance pp. 160f.); on this see the critique of J. Jeremias, *Jerusalem zur Zeit Jesu* Vol. II, p. 116 n., although his identification of Pharisees and *Hasidim* on the basis of 1 Macc. ii. 42 is not quite accurate (p. 116); he wishes to understand them as a priestly opposition group directed against the Sadducees (pp. 138f).

[28] P. Volz, *Die Eschatologie der jüdischen Gemeinde im neutestamentlichen Zeitalter* (1934), p. 10: 'The Rabbinic theologians regarded apocalyptic as an enthusiastic type of piety and saw in this a danger to morality; the pessimistic-dualistic viewpoint struck them as inflated; although they did not deny the connection of sin and evil with Satan and demons, they emphasized the power of the moral will and the necessity of moral awareness. Further, they considered the closed secret circle as an offence against society.' They had the mentality of a spiritual ruler-élite, who no longer needed to fear for their dominating position and who could present themselves in a conservative and emphatically responsible light.

CHAPTER IV

ANALYSIS OF SELECTED ESCHATOLOGICAL PASSAGES

1. THE ISAIAH-APOCALYPSE (Isa. xxiv–xxvii)

A FULL discussion of the 'Isaiah-Apocalypse' (Isa. xxiv–xxvii), which has been the subject of many separate studies,[1] cannot be undertaken here. There are numerous interpretations already in existence: namely, as to whether Isa. xxiv–xxvii is a combination of eschatological prophecies and later psalms[2] or an earlier collection of psalms about an anonymous city, expanded and enriched by apocalyptic prophecies (Eissfeldt, *Introduction*, p. 326), or a prophetic liturgy[3] confined to ch. xxv and xxvi, or a sort of cantata, consisting, after the excision of secondary parts, of antiphonal, eschatological poems together with some psalms,[4] or a collection of different psalms, the majority of which derive from the same author[5]; it is not our intention to add to this number yet another interpretation of similar form by seeking to make use of some of the correct insights of previous studies; Eissfeldt's warning (*Introduction*, p. 326) against restricting oneself to any single interpretation should be heeded with profit— and not only here.

Our starting point, which is certainly not new, is the conviction that the 'Isaiah-Apocalypse'[6] occupies a clearly marked, distinctive position at the end of the foreign oracles of Isaiah (Isa. xiii–xxiii) prior to a further collection of ancient sayings of Isaiah (Isa. xxviiif.). We are not dealing with oracles of the prophet Isaiah[7]; nor is it a collection of prophetic oracles, dealing with a particular people or city in the manner of the preceding oracles against foreign nations.

---

[1] Further literature in O. Eissfeldt, *The Old Testament: an Introduction*; for separate studies see particularly p. 756, O. Ludwig, *Die Stadt in der Jesaja-Apokalypse. Zur Deutung von Jes.* 24–27 (Diss. Bonn, 1961).
[2] B. Duhm, *Das Buch Jesaja*, HAT 3 no. 1 (1922⁴).
[3] G. Hylmö, *De s.k. profetiska liturgiernas rytm, stil och komposition I Jes.* xxv. 1–xxvi. 21 (1929).
[4] J. Lindblom, *Die Jesaja-Apokalypse. Jes.* 24–27 (1938).
[5] W. Rudolph, *Jes.* 24–27 (1933). Mention should also be made of the dissertation of E. S. Mulder, *Die Teologie van die Jesaja-Apokalipse Jes.* 24–27 (Diss. Gronigen, 1954), which I was not able to examine before my own manuscript was complete.
[6] This description is not very appropriate, but it has established itself and may, therefore, be retained; for a critique of the term cf. Lindblom, pp. 102ff.
[7] The most important reasons against the authenticity of Isa. xxiv–xxvii have been collected by Rudolph; cf. pp. 6of.

The only concrete indication which might be urged in favour of this, the reference to Moab in xxv. 10, makes it immediately obvious upon comparison with the Moab-sayings in Isa. xv and xvi that we can hardly explain the composition of Isa. xxiv–xxvii by means of a Moab oracle which has been greatly expanded at a later date. If, in fact, an ancient saying against Moab did give the impetus to the formation of the apocalypse, this source has been ignored so completely that it could hardly have been important for the growth of the present collection and for the special position of Isa. xxiv–xxvii. We cannot, however, compare this little book with the preceding oracles against the nations; instead we must regard it as a distinctive section, resting on a distinctive development.

An overall survey of the contents[8] reveals a remarkable juxtaposition of prophecies—understanding this primarily in a general sense—and psalms; this, therefore, may be taken as the starting point for our analysis of the apocalypse. The two series, of course, are not unrelated to each other; in fact, one has the impression that they have been linked on the principle of alternation, so that the view that we are dealing with an ordered composition is readily intelligible. But this arrangement has clearly been superimposed; for some of the psalms, e.g. the psalms of thanksgiving in xxv. 1f. and xxvi. 1f., which are related by content, refer to a victory already achieved by Yahweh in an anonymous city and have only been assimilated to the dominant future perspective by their present position or, in the second instance, by a remark prefaced in xxvi. 1a. Originally there need not have been any 'eschatological' hymns. But this futuristic outlook—we may call it 'eschatological' if we mean by this primarily a definitive pattern of relationships expected in the future—obviously became the dominant view that contributed substantially to the present shape of the apocalypse. We are justified, therefore, in beginning with the prophetic passages.

It should be added that not all parts of the apocalypse can be fitted into the above two types (prophecies and psalms) of tradition (e.g. the reflective meditation in xxvi. 7–11, which is quite separate from the following unit in xxvi. 12f., which has the form of a lament) and that, in addition, the two series are by no means complete in themselves. The psalm in xxvii. 2f. diverges considerably from the psalm of thanksgiving referred to above and the psalm inserted in xxiv. 8f., which describes the desolation of a city that has been

---

[8] For the textual difficulties, which are not negligible, the reader may be referred to existing commentaries and monographs.

annihilated, cannot at once be brought into line with the psalms of thanksgiving in xxv and xxvi. Similarly the prophetic passages also do not form a self-contained unit, but seem like extended or abridged reflections from a more comprehensive repertoire.

In comparison with the remaining chapters, xxiv seems fairly uniform in so far as it is completely dominated by the future perspective. It begins in participial style without any of the references to chronology which usually occur in eschatological sections; it seeks to express something immediate that has no chronological limitation by declaring that Yahweh will destroy the earth. This destructive activity of Yahweh is described in words of the same root in Nahum ii. 11, while the enumeration in xxiv. 2 is reminiscent of Hos. iv. 4 and 9; in fact, the beginning of Hos. iv must have exercised an influence on our passage in other respects also.[9] There is a striking affirmation in xxiv. 3 that Yahweh has spoken, although no word of Yahweh has been recorded either preceding (as in Isa. i. 20) or following (as in Isa. i. 2). If the final clause, which may have undergone secondary expansion, is not to be taken as a figure of speech, it should be reflected that such a remark, the addition of which was certainly not unintentional, was made possible by the use of certain prophetic passages which were regarded as words of Yahweh: the view put forward here about the destruction of the world certainly does not claim to be *communis opinio* but aims to draw upon the sphere of Yahweh's revelation, which clearly includes both *Torah* (Gen. ix) and prophetic writings, for they are complementary. God's action in xxiv. 1 and 3 is followed by the result in xxiv. 4, together with a reason in xxiv. 5f., to ward off any suspicion that Yahweh is acting capriciously; man's guilt is clearly emphasized. The conclusion is reached with the statement that the number of survivors will be negligible (cf. the twice repeated '*al-kol* in xxiv. 6). Isa. xxiv. 1–6, which includes both introduction and theme, speaks universally of the future judgment of the world and mankind, and has in view the primeval history in the form we know it—the influence of the Priestly Writing is undeniable—and bases its futuristic outlook on certain prophetic traditions. It is not evident, however, what gave rise to the treatment of such a theme. Anticipating, we might add that even the following unit xxiv. 7–13 does not disclose this.[10]

[9] Cf. for instance the transgression of the commandments which are reminiscent of the Decalogue and the effect of this on creation in Hos. iv. 2f. with the breach of the 'eternal covenant' (Gen. ix.) and with the resulting consequences in Isa. xxiv. 4f.
[10] But cf. Rudolph, p. 9 and Lindblom, p. 14.

This second section, consisting mainly of vv. 8–12, is independent of xxiv. 1–6. It tells how the wine runs out and mirth is stilled in a destroyed 'city of chaos'. It is quite natural to connect this originally independent poem about a desolate city with the other poems which also mention a destroyed city (xxv. 1f. and xxvi. 1f.); but it should not be overlooked that the general tenor of this poem is very different. Instead of triumph that the city has been destroyed, there is a note of mourning and sympathy, because joyless desolation has taken the place of happiness and mirth; hence the psalm may be interpreted throughout as a psalm of lament.[11] That the psalm of lament became a lampoon on the lips of the Jews (so Lindblom following Lohmann) may be true in other cases, but finds no support in the present text. This psalm, in contrast to the psalms in xxv. 1f. and xxvi. 1f., should obviously not be thought of as independent; whatever its original context, in its present position it forms the detailed continuation of xxiv. 1f. Thus, there is no indication at the beginning of it that we are dealing here with a new unit, such as we noticed, for instance, in xxvi. 1; on the contrary, in fact, the verbs in xxiv. 7 deliberately pick up xxiv. 4. Obviously xxiv. 7 is a bridge-passage, stemming from the author of xxiv. 1–6 and set in a psalm that was originally independent but has not been fully preserved; this psalm was clearly distinct from the psalms in xxv and xxvi, with which it has only apparent connection. The author of xxiv. 1–6, in order to continue his description, has emphasized one graphic feature with the aim of speaking to the general condition of his contemporaries. The reference is no longer to a particular city, whose destruction is hinted at, but to the city life of contemporary civilization in general, which Yahweh's destructive activity will not by-pass. Rudolph has rightly perceived that the concluding sentence, xxiv. 13, is connected with the final verse of xxiv. 6; but his attempt to use the fragment xxiv. 8–12 as an independent unit has unfortunately caused him to connect xxiv. 13 immediately with xxiv. 6. Isa. xxiv. 13, however, is to be treated like xxiv. 7; it is a concluding remark, rounding off and summarizing the previous sections; it contains a reference perhaps to Isa. xvii. 6 and seeks to prove in connection with xxiv. 6b that the multiplication of men under the divine blessing (a further reminder of Gen. ix) has been replaced by reduction in the numbers of men because of the curse.

There is no justification, therefore, for excising any verses as an

---

[11] So Lindblom (p. 19), following P. Lohmann, 'Die selbständigen lyrischen Abschnitte in Jes. 24–27', *ZAW* 18 (1917), pp. 1f.

independent unit, even though they were undoubtedly independent once, for they have been made an integral part of the narrative by the author of our chapter. Thus, the section xxiv. 8–12, together with the bridge-verses 7 and 13, is to be interpreted as a continuation of xxiv. 1–6.

In considering the following verses, xxiv. 14f., it is important to notice that in xxiv. 18b–20 the narrative picks up the opening verses of the chapter, beginning with a reference to the catastrophe of the Flood and leading to a preliminary ending in xxiv. 19f. Thus, the quotation from Amos v. 2 at the end of xxiv. 20 may have an 'unfortunate' effect (Duhm, p. 152); but it may be excused as a preliminary conclusion. It illustrates the somewhat hopeless attempt to prophesy future events in accordance with honoured, recorded sayings of the earlier prophets.

The intermediate verses, xxiv. 14–18a, are determined by a contrast, which in view of the obscure word *hemmah* in xxiv. 14 it is not easy to explicate. Lindblom objects that Rudolph, by placing xxiv. 13 immediately after xxiv. 6, has left *hemmah* unrelated; he therefore links xxiv. 14 closely with xxiv. 13 and sees in *hemmah* Palestinian Jews, who regard themselves according to xxiv. 13 as unimportant gleanings and who now join with all who are summoned to praise God in singing the mighty deeds of Yahweh, namely the destruction of the 'city of chaos' of xxiv. 10. In that case, however, the cry of woe in xxiv. 16b cannot be joined with it. Accordingly Lindblom omits *wa'omar* in xxiv. 16b as a secondary link-word and relates the cry of woe to the eschatological catastrophe which was spoken of at the beginning of the chapter and which was described again in xxiv. 18b onwards. This, however, means the complete loss of the obvious contrast between xxiv. 14 (*hemmah*) and xxiv. 16b (*wa'omar*). Rudolph, it seems, attributes no special significance to the word *hemmah* and translates, 'they raise their voices . . . 'The LXX, however, considered it necessary to define *hemmah* more precisely (*hoi kataleiphthentes tes ges*) and drew on xxiv. 13 for this purpose. The meaning of *hemmah* must be understood from the contrast with *wa'omar*; a double *hemmah-hemmah* would have been clearer, but this was not possible since *hemmah* on the one side was balanced by an individual on the other side. Hence, the correct translation is, 'Others raise their voices and rejoice in the majesty of Yahweh . . . but I must say . . .' (so, too, Rudolph, following Procksch[12]). There is nothing to suggest that the jubilation is caused

[12] O. Procksch, *Jesaja I*, KAT IX no. 1 (1930), loc. cit.

E

by the destruction of the city referred to in xxiv. 10; it is based on wider events, namely on the eschatological activity of Yahweh, which has so far been discussed as a whole. Those who are rejoicing obviously do not come into the category of those earth-dwellers who have broken the 'everlasting covenant' and have evoked the judgement of Yahweh. Those who are rejoicing, therefore, must refer to the Jews, including the whole Diaspora, who are aware of their exceptional position and regard themselves as the righteous who share in glory (xxiv. 16a).

The objection in xxiv. 16b is raised by an individual; but this individual figure is obviously conscious of being one of a group of like-minded people, so that the first person plural in xxiv. 16a (*šāma'nu*) should not be altered. The point of the objection should be evident[13]: the author is protesting against the superficial view, which expresses itself in premature joy as a result of preliminary, pre-eschatological events and thus detracts from the eschatological activity of Yahweh. It should be noticed, however, that, before he proceeds with his description of the destruction of the world in xxiv. 18b and seeks to emphasize the gruesomeness, and in fact uniqueness, of the catastrophe in contrast to what was said in xxiv. 1–3, the author clothes his protest in xxiv. 16b–18a in formulae which were derived from completely different contexts and could hardly be regarded as displaying a happy grasp of the repertoire of ancient threats of judgement, although there are turns of phrase and similes taken from the prophetic books.[14] The author clearly sets great store on being able to support his protest with the words of recognized prophets; this is the way in which the eschatological picture is built up. With xxiv. 20 a certain terminus is reached; the following unit is given emphasis by means of an introductory formula and embraces vv. 21–3. It stands in a looser relationship to the other verses in the chapter and seems to be fairly independent; consideration of it may be postponed on a first survey of xxiv. 1–20.

The section we have looked at so far is undoubtedly fairly uniform. It begins and ends with the prophecy of destruction on a universal scale; the introduction of the prophecy is mild by comparison with its conclusion. The prophecy is based on the sketch of primeval history in Gen. i–xi, but uses in addition phrases from the prophetic books. An originally independent psalm, the historical situation of which is no longer clear, has been inserted in its present context by

---

[13] On the interpretation of xxiv. 16 bα cf. Rudolph, p. 12.
[14] Cf. xxiv. 16b with Isa. xxi. 2; xxiv. 17f. with Jer. xlviii. 43 and Amos. v. 19.

means of two verses at the beginning and end, with the obvious intention of reviving the prophecy of judgement for the contemporary world, the life of which is determined by urban civilization. The motivation for this eschatological conception is perhaps to be sought in vv. 14–18a. This passage is at pains to emphasize the eschatological aspect and is a protest against premature rejoicing, which, being convinced of Israel's unique position, expects visible confirmation of this in unimportant events and thus threatens to detract from the eschatological event. The author of our section is also convinced of Israel's unique position, but he speaks for a like-minded group (xxiv. 16: šāmaʿnu) of an eschatological catastrophe of cosmic dimension, the scale and extent of which he tries to delineate by means of expressions taken from the prophetic tradition with which he was familiar (xxiv. 16b–18a). This piece of eschatological nonconformity is the centre of the passage we have been discussing; compared with superficial, and therefore ultimately ineffective, eschatological expectation the severity of eschatological catastrophe must be taken seriously.

In spite of this emphasis upon the eschatological aspect there was probably no need to stress the position of Israel particularly, since it was presumably beyond all doubt. If such an emphasis is to be found in xxiv. 21–3, an independent addition, it must have ensued at a later date, when the reason which led to the meditation in xxiv. 1–20 was no longer so important or a different reason had made its appearance, so that it seemed desirable to have a complete picture of the future including Israel. Possibly the catch-word m^erom (xxiv. 4 and 18) played a part in this. Further, the disarmament of heavenly and earthly powers (xxiv. 21) could easily be linked with the cosmic scope of judgement. Whether 'host of heaven' refers to astral deities (Lindblom) or angels that guide terrestrial nations as in the Book of Daniel (Rudolph) depends on our interpretation of v. 23a; the confusion of sun and moon can be taken as a sort of disarmament, although it may simply be the result of the cosmic change (cf. for instance Jonah iii. 4; Isa. lx. 19; Zech. xiv. 6f.). The two lines of interpretation should not be separated too sharply[15]; in later apocalypses first one, then the other interpretation has pre-eminence.[16] xxiv. 22 poses no small textual difficulty; xxiv. 22a is obviously thinking of the disarmament and captivity of Yahweh's

[15] Cf. Lindblom, p. 28, whereas Rudolph (p. 33) follows the interpretation of the Book of Daniel, which may also reproduce the interpretation of an earlier period.
[16] Cf. the importance of the angelic patrons of the nations in the Book of Daniel, and the conflict of the angels with the stars in Enoch (Enoch xc. 24; cf. also 18f.).

opponents who are referred to in xxiv. 21, whereas xxiv. 22b refers to their final punishment, which is distinct in time from their disarmament. This need not be understood in the sense of a double judgement, however; the repetition of *pkd* (xxiv. 21 and 22b) indicates that it refers to an eschatological event which falls into two acts, in which the chronological reference in xxiv. 22b has a formal appearance and seems to have been chosen deliberately. The eschatological drama, which has entered its decisive, final phase in the independent addition xxiv. 21–3, opens with the disarmament of the enemy and closes with the epiphany of Yahweh on Mount Zion before the representatives of Israel, who are pointedly called 'the elders of Yahweh' (cf. Rudolph, p. 34), a reference back to Exod. xxiv. 9f. (P). The inclusion of Israel in the epiphany of Yahweh is an integral part of Yahweh's lordship, which, in view of the cosmic catastrophe and the disarmament of earthly kings of other nations in xxiv. 21b, needs to be supplemented with an account of how it will affect these other nations whose rulers have been disarmed. As frequently emphasized in the past, this is dealt with in xxv. 6–8, a section which in comparison with xxiv. 21–23, and indeed with the rest of ch. xxiv, is undoubtedly thought of as independent and at the same time as a continuation of xxiv. 23.[17] Thus, a certain lapse of time may be presumed between the events in xxiv. 21–23 and the great banquet of nations in xxv. 6–8; this is prepared for by the formal phrase *merob yamim* in xxiv. 22b. Chronologically, therefore, the final judgement on the enemies of Yahweh would coincide with the great banquet of joy for the nations.

We shall pass over the psalm of thanksgiving in xxv. 1–5 to begin with and consider xxv. 6–8 in immediate connection with xxiv. 21–23. The prophecy of the great banquet of joy on Zion ends in xxv. 8 without any mention of God's word, such as the final phrase would lead us to expect. With the account of the banquet, the removal of mourning garb and the drying of all tears we reach the climax of Yahweh's epiphany, but not without a concluding sentence underlining Israel's privilege; the meal shared with foreign nations is also

---

[17] That the two sections are independent may be inferred from the outward form also. xxiv. 21–23 does not reveal any marked metrical structure and is best regarded as exalted prose, whereas xxv. 6–8 seems to be more definitely metrical, although the restoration of metrical form requires some textual emendations. The metrical analysis of Isa. xxiv attempted by Procksch and Lindblom following Sievers certainly supports the view that we are dealing at times with independent units even within larger contexts. It strengthens the conviction that in the eschatological part of the Isaiah-Apocalypse we have before us a narrative which goes back to sayings derived from other contexts. They are 'eschatologoumena' from a traditional repertoire, which there were reasons for not wishing to bypass.

a rehabilitation for the people of Zion. The short clause in xxv. 8aα referring to the abolition of death is fittingly transferred by Rudolph to stand directly before the final phrase of xxv. 8, and thus its character as a gloss, which its present position undoubtedly gives it, is to some extent removed; but in that case the mention of death is less appropriate. Since the passage is dealing with the destiny and future of nations and peoples rather than the fate and death of the individual, a remark to the effect that death is swallowed up does not seem appropriate to the original context of this section. Hence the clause should probably be regarded as a gloss from the hand of a later writer, providing continuity and interpretation (so Lindblom and almost all previous commentators, although Procksch, Hylmö and Rudolph try to retain the clause). There is also a measure of inconsistency in referring to many nations in connection with the eschatological pilgrimage of the nations to Mount Zion (Isa. ii), when according to xxiv. 6 there are only a few survivors from the cosmic catastrophe; but we are dealing with independent units and occasional inconsistencies are not felt to be disruptive, an observation which also applies to historical books in the Old Testament. In addition, Rudolph and Lindblom rightly point to the haphazard way in which eschatological traditions are often strung together. It is, of course, in the nature of every eschatology that it should be unwilling to bring the separate traits of hopes and expectations under a common denominator. The reason for this is that a systematic eschatology devoted to the personal expectation of the individual, which should always be regarded as the strongest impulse behind eschatological ideas, does not give sufficient scope and stunts any real expectation; for, although a living hope requires general lines of guidance by which to find its bearings, it is reluctant to submit to dogmatic regimentation. The following consideration, however, strikes me as even more important. The description of the eschatological catastrophe, especially in xxiv. 1–6 and 17–20, picks up older traditions, although it uses and arranges them freely. For the final phase of the eschatological drama, which also concerns the fate of Israel, it uses independent units, which are taken over as they stand; this enables it to display reserve in formulating its own views and to emphasize its agreement with an existing eschatological tradition.

The eschatological banquet undoubtedly forms the climax of the description; no further development is to be expected. In fact, this brings us to the end of the description of eschatological events, which consists of consecutive but independent units. The only other passage belonging here is xxvi. 20f., an admonitory conclusion. But the intervening units in xxv. 9–xxvi. 19 should not be passed over as secondary; although they pursue different aims, some parts at least have considerable significance for the total narrative.

Up to the end of ch. xxv we are dealing with a number of independent sections of the most diverse types. The first unit stretches from xxv. 9 to xxv. 10a; it is impossible to reckon with a continuation of the brief expression of confidence beyond this point. For *bahar hazzeh* points back beyond xxv. 8 to xxiv. 21–23, and Rudolph's attempt to link xxv. 12 directly with xxv. 10a had already aroused Lindblom's misgiving (p. 39). xxv. 12 is best regarded as an expansion of the Moab saying in xxv. 10b–xxv. 11, which was felt to be too brief; it is based on xxvi. 5. But xxv. 9 and 10a are equally independent, as is clear from the introductory formula in xxv. 9; hence they are not to be linked too closely with xxv. 6–8, as Lindblom suggests. It is an expression of trust in the form of a short hymn of thanksgiving, able to tell of the protection and care of Yahweh in the present because of the special significance which Zion possesses in the eschatological event. Thus, the brief hymn of thanksgiving may be understood as the response of those who have hope, who are willing to go to meet the coming catastrophe in reliance upon Yahweh; the unique significance of Mount Zion accounts for Israel's exemption from the eschatological catastrophe, which is not indicated in the present text of the initial verses of ch. xxiv.

Along with the majority of commentators the brief Moab saying in xxv. 10b and 11, later expanded by xxv. 12, is to be regarded as a secondary insertion. Eissfeldt (*Introduction*, p. 326) rightly rejects Torrey's attempt to give the Moab saying a more general colour by altering *mo'ab* in v. 10a to *'oyeb* and thus bring it into keeping with the eschatological perspective. But Eissfeldt's own view, which draws attention to the statements directed against Moab in Isa. xv f and the analogy with Isa. xxxiv and xxxv (a catastrophe over Edom is eschatologically expanded into a universal catastrophe), offers insufficient basis, it seems to me, for understanding the origin of the whole Isaiah-Apocalypse in a similar manner; the eschatological perspective must have been determinative for the apocalypse as a whole from the beginning. Agreement with Eissfeldt is possible to the extent that the psalm in xxiv. 8–12, which was originally independent, but which has been deprived of its independence and fitted into the eschatological narrative, can be linked with a catastrophe on one of the cities of vine-growing Moab in view of the importance of wine for the city described there; the memory of this may perhaps explain the insertion of the Moab saying in xxv. 10b and 11 at a later date. But all local references have been completely removed from the poem in xxiv. 8–12 and it has been made part of the eschatological description. We shall probably have to be content with the information that a historical event which can no longer be reconstructed in detail has occasioned the secondary insertion of the Moab saying together with a later expansion of it in xxv. 12.

If, then, we leave the Moab sayings on one side and regard the brief hymn of thanksgiving in xxv. 9 and 10a as the trusting response of the 'community' to the announcement of the eschatological catastrophe, and we also—to anticipate—wish to include the final admonition of xxvi. 20f. in the eschatological part of our apocalypse, then the transition from the hymn of thanksgiving in xxv. 9 and 10a to this closing admonition in xxvi. 20f. remains unexplained. Nor can any justification be found in the psalm in xxvi. 1b–6, which the superscription in xxvi. 1a denotes as independent. We have already postponed consideration of a similar psalm in xxv. 1–5 until later and propose to do the same with this second psalm in xxvi. 1f. xxvi. 7f. would then be connected directly with xxv. 10a, and the reason for the admonition in xxvi. 20f. after the brief hymn of thanksgiving in xxv. 9 and 10a would have to be sought in xxvi. 7–19. In fact, within the eschatological description this section xxvi. 7–19 seems to be *sui generis*.

The internal structure of this extensive section is interpreted very differently. To mention but a few views, whereas Duhm regards the whole passage xxvi. 1–19 as a very 'artificial' poem (p. 158) and does not distinguish it at all sharply from the hymn in xxvi. 1–6, Rudolph thinks he can recognize a fairly self-contained unit from xxvi. 7, although it is not marked by any regularity of strophe structure (pp. 46f.); but he would like to be able to exclude xxvi. 14a, 18bβ, 19 as an independent unit, because it deals with resurrection from the dead, and would prefer to see some important transpositions in such an edited version of the poem (xxvi. 13 and 14b behind xxvi 18, followed immediately by xxvi. 20f.). Lindblom tries to link xxvi. 7–14 with the previous psalm xxvi. 1–6 and to interpret xxvi. 15–19 as an independent psalm of lament (pp. 40f. with a brief survey of the various interpretations), which should be omitted from the Isaiah-Apocalypse as a later insertion (pp. 66f.). The most common view, however, may be summed up in Eissfeldt's words (*Introduction*, p. 324); xxvi. 7–19 contains a 'prayer rather like a national lament, asking for the removal of the distress which is oppressing the people, and which it cannot avert of itself, and for the restoration to life of dead compatriots', to which a swift response is promised in the divine answer in xxvi. 20f., which follows the prayer. Even if we leave out of consideration for the moment the question whether xxvi. 20f. should be regarded as the conclusion of a larger unit, this attitude of prayer characterizes the whole section; only in xxvi. 19 is there conceivably a word of Yahweh, as Rudolph suggests and as Hylmö had felt before him; but Rudolph connects xxvi. 19 directly with xxvi. 14a and xxvi. 18bβ as a distinct unit, which is concerned with the question of resurrection from the dead, and ascribes it to a later hand. But the possibility that xxvi. 19 is an oracle of Yahweh rounding off vv. 7–19 should not be rejected out of hand.

Apart from xxvi. 19 the section xxvi. 7–18 may be understood as a combination of two units with a break after xxvi. 11. For the first unit xxvi. 7–11 Lindblom's description could be taken over, although I differ considerably from his analysis of the passage as a whole. 'What follows in xxvi. 7 is the creed-like description of Yahweh's activity in general terms: God always makes level the path of the righteous. The theme continues in xxvi. 9b: the inhabitants of the world learn what God's righteousness is from his judgements on earth. The reliance on Wisdom material is unmistakeable. This is even more pronounced in what follows: the godless do not learn righteousness, on earth they distort truth and pass away without perceiving the revelation of Yahweh's glory ... Hope in the future, which is expressed so beautifully in Ps. xl. 12, finds expression here also in typical phrases, namely in xxvi. 8f.: we wait for thee, our desire is for thy name, my soul yearns for thee in the night, and my spirit longs for thee. This waiting for Yahweh may also be regarded as the substance of the typical confession of faith found in psalms of thanksgiving' (pp. 41f.). I have quoted Lindblom's words at length because I agree with them wholeheartedly, but wish to suggest a different interpretation; it is not accidental that Lindblom's interpretation is restricted to vv. 7–11, although he thinks the section reaches to the end of v. 14.

The contrast between the righteous and the godless which is well-known from many psalms and from the wisdom literature occupies an equally central position as the waiting upon Yahweh. But within an eschatological meditation, such as the present verses belong to through their connection with xxv. 10a, this very familiar theme must have particular significance, just as the waiting upon Yahweh

must also be considered from a particular point of view. Duhm
(p. 160) regards the speaker as the representative (chorus leader) of
the strict Pharisaic group with which he identifies himself, a view
which is to be understood in the light of the late date of origin
(Maccabean-Hasmonaean) recommended by Duhm for the verses
under consideration. For him the godless are the Gentiles and pagan-
minded Jews, who insult Yahweh's majesty by their disobedience
to the Law. This, at any rate, is probably correct in Duhm's exposition, namely, that the issue here is a contemporary difference, which
is described by means of general expressions from the Psalms and
Wisdom literature, but has in mind a definite conflict. In an eschatological passage it can only concern a difference in the sphere
affected by eschatological expectations. Thus, the paths of the
righteous, the judgements of Yahweh and waiting upon Yahweh
become phrases pregnant with significance: they concern the path
of the man who is righteous because the goal of his journey is the
eschatological millenium; hence, the judgements of Yahweh already
proclaim this goal to the man of insight, and the peculiar tension
of waiting for Yahweh consists in the fact that it refers to waiting
for the epiphany of Yahweh. On the other hand, the eyes of the
earth-dweller may be opened when the divine judgements begin;
he will learn righteousness, i.e. insight into the coming events, in
the same sense, for instance, as the eschatological 'teachers' in the
Book of Daniel are said to have led many to righteousness (Dan.
xii. 3). The godless, however, is clearly separated from the righteous
and from the earth-dweller; he occupies the position of those who
are called *marši'e berit* in Dan. xi. 32; what was meant by transgression of the covenant at a time of religious conflict, referred, at
this undoubtedly earlier period, to disobedience in the sense of
doubting or not paying attention to eschatological conviction. Such
a transgressor will not learn righteousness in the sense of eschatological insight and will, therefore, have no share in the greatness of
Yahweh which will be revealed at his eschatological epiphany. He
will be regarded as Yahweh's enemy when Yahweh takes up the
cause of his people who have remained steadfast to the eschatological
faith; and the fire which is the fate of Yahweh's enemies will destroy
him.

It is clear, then, that we are dealing with a division within the
Jewish community. The transgressors are certainly not those mentioned in xxiv. 14, who rejoice rashly and prematurely and see the
great turning-point in insignificant historical events, thus emptying

the eschatological faith of its importance and assisting the disbelief and rejection of this faith. Those referred to here are those who have already fallen prey to this scepticism and who—continuing the line to the Book of Daniel—in the times of testing are among those who transgress the covenant of Yahweh. This internal division is described in traditional language familiar to us from the Psalms and Wisdom literature; its use here, however, is eschatologically motivated. Apparently this division has not yet assumed hard and fast proportions; the contours are still fluid, because we are dealing with a theological difference before it has begun to alter the contemporary confession of faith. There are probably rallying points of this division in the case of transgressors and righteous alike, which conceal a more or less visible association; but it would probably be wrong to assume any rigid division within the community as a whole at this stage. It seems to me worthwhile to investigate this variance that is revealed by xxvi. 7f. for the causes that led to the formation and development of our apocalypse, which then became a prayer-book for the eschatological groups, a handbook to strengthen their personal faith by its distinctive eschatological structure, and a work of apologetic against their opponents. It seems to me, therefore, quite mistaken to wish to exclude this section from the apocalypse; it forms the heart of the narrative, insofar as it gives us an insight into the situation in which our short book received its present shape—a time when hope in the eschatological millenium was by no means taken for granted by all the members of the community, and in fact frequently encountered doubt even in eschatological circles.

The second part of our section, namely, vv. 12–18, seems to wish to do justice to this last point. Here again a live question is at issue, but its significance is esoteric. The discussion is restricted to 'the righteous' and aims to strengthen those who are struggling with temptation. As far as the textual difficulties are concerned I can give broad support to the suggested emendations of Rudolph, although I would not exclude the verses which deal with the resurrection of the dead and make them a separate, independent unit (xxvi. 14a, 18bβ, 19); for that reason his transpositions of verses strike me as too severe an interference with the text; his alteration of the third person plural into the first person plural in xxvi. 16 also seems unnecessary to me, because the section is characterized by a combination of past and present, so that no sharp distinction is made between earlier generations and the present generation. xxvi. 12 contains an expression of trust, a resolve to wait for salvation from Yahweh alone, while in xxvi. 13 the speaker surveys the past and identifies himself with his people in earlier centuries and in general terms calls to mind the periods of foreign domination. Consequently, like the eyes of the prophet in Ezek. xxxvii, his view glides over the graveyard of his people in history. But he is able to make brief reference to the peaks as well as to the depths in this history. The statement in xxvi. 15 about the people multiplying and the borders being enlarged is not to be understood in the sense of a chronological 'consequence' in relation to xxvi. 13; it is a general reference to the great peaks of Israelite history, which have been brought about by Yahweh, as for instance xxvi. 16 recalls the attitude of the Israelites in the difficult days of the Judges: Yahweh, in distress they sought thee out. The affliction of magic was their punishment from thee. He does not delve further; for he had reached the point to which he could link his present situation; hence, the first person plural in xxvi. 17b and 18 is designed to embrace the Israel of past and present. The reading xxvi. 18b, 17, 18 creates difficulties for me, however; like a woman with child, who writhes and cries out in her pangs, so were we, Yahweh, before thee. We were with child, we writhed in pain—k^emo should be excised—we brought forth wind; we did not achieve anything for the earth and no one fell (i.e. was born). The two sentences in xxvi. 18b are parallel; the second sentence, therefore, must be a figurative repetition of the first, resuming the picture of the woman with child in xxvi. 17 and paving the way for the divine oracle in xxvi. 19. The pains of the woman with child have only one meaning, insofar as they accompany the birth of someone: our pains and woes, the verse is saying, have accomplished nothing; we have not 'given birth' to anyone, i.e. we have had no visible results. It is not a question of desire for the multiplication of the people, as is often readily assumed, but of the advent of salvation; the woes and pains are metaphors taken over from xxvi. 17 to describe the writhing between hope and disappointment. This indicates the straits in which the eschatological groups at that time found themselves. Their doubt about the accuracy of the eschatological faith is terminated by Yahweh's word in xxvi. 19. But this answer does not support a desired increase of the population so that the dead arise to take the place of those who are missing. Rather, the resurrection of the dead is introduced as the visible expression of the great eschatological turning-point; hence it is the visible termination of the inner struggle with temptation of those who are conscious of their debt to the eschatological faith. This postulate of the resurrection of the dead as a visible sign that things have come to an end is taken over by the Book of Daniel in ch. xii for the purpose of encouraging those who have remained loyal to their eschatological conviction and hence to the covenant with Yahweh at a time when testing has already been found necessary.

Thus xxvi. 20f. immediately suggests itself as the conclusion of the preceding eschatological passage; for xxvi. 21 clearly picks up xxiv. 20, whilst including in 'the dead' what has been said in connection with the resurrection of the dead in xxvi. 12f. It does not seem wise, therefore, to look for a continuation of this brief exhortation of the 'prophet'[18] beyond xxvi. 21 or to interpret xxvi. 20f. as the beginning of another description of cosmic judgement, as Rudolph (p. 49) does, together with the addition of xxvii. 1 and xxvii. 12f. Chap. xxvii can be left out of account in the interpretation of the preceding parts of the apocalypse. The admonition in xxvi. 20f. makes good sense after the reflection in xxvi. 7f., which was concluded by the divine oracle. We find the same warning addressed to Daniel in the final verse of the Book of Daniel (xii. 13); hence it would be quite possible to think of the 'chambers' in xxvi. 20, in which the people are to hide themselves, as graves. The admonition would then take on the pointed sense of suffering death because its allotted duration will be short-lived, and the insertion of the gloss in xxv. 8aα (the abolition of death) would be understandable in connection with the eschatological treatment. But since there is no proof of the meaning 'grave' for *hdr* in the Old Testament—it always refers to particularly private rooms of the house[19]—it is better to disregard this interpretation. There may, however, be a general reference to the Temple, the smaller rooms of which are sometimes described by *hdr* (1 Chron. xxviii. 11). Whatever the exact truth of this, the verse takes for granted that those addressed know where they are to retire to when the eschatological crisis begins. This also tacitly assumes that such a place of refuge will not be overtaken by the destructive activity of Yahweh.

Before turning our attention to ch. xxvii, a brief consideration of the psalms in xxv. 1f. and xxvi. 1f., which have been passed over so far, must be appended; they concern an unnamed city. We are dealing only with these two passages; for the poem in xxiv. 8–12, which also refers to a nameless city, has now come to be regarded as

---

[18] Hylmö considers xxvi. 20 a continuation of God's utterance in xxvi. 19; this can hardly be right. Cf. on this Rudolph, p. 50 n. 17.

[19] The master's room (Gen. xliii. 30; Judges xvi. 9 etc.); the bedchamber (Exod. vii. 28; 1 Sam. iv. 7 etc.); the women's room (Judges xv. 1. etc.).

part of the eschatological narrative as a result of the transitions in xxiv. 7 and 13, although it is quite distinct from the surrounding verses and must have been an independent unit originally; originally, too, it pursued quite different aims from the hymns of thanksgiving in ch. xxv-xxvi by reason of its tone of lament mingled with sympathy. While xxv. 12 also refers to a city, it is to be understood as a secondary and very confused expansion of the Moab saying, which was inserted later, and is composed of parts of the two hymns of thanksgiving in ch. xxv and xxvi.[20] (For xxvii. 10aα reference should be made to the discussion of ch. xxvii). In contrast, the psalms in xxv. 1-5 and xxvi. 1-6 are not only independent and distinct from the surrounding verses; they should also be interpreted separately and independently. In the case of xxvi. 1 this is particularly emphasized by the superscription, whilst in xxv. 1 it can be clearly seen in the external form of address to Yahweh. Neither psalm has anything to do with the eschatological narrative. It is inconceivable that the mighty deed of Yahweh that is magnified in the psalms as a historical event was later expanded point by point into an eschatological cosmic catastrophe—the reference to corresponding parallels in the prophetic literature are not fully convincing[21]—nor can the two psalms be considered analogous to the psalm inserted in ch. xxiv dealing with what was once a city of wine and mirth. In fact, it seems to me, it is not even certain that the same city must be meant in the two psalms (of ch. xxv and xxvi). For the psalm in ch. xxv the view that Babylon is meant, suggested by Lindblom and Rudolph among others, may be correct; for the psalm in ch. xxvi an important, fortified city should probably be thought of, but one that is to be sought nearer to Palestine. Perhaps this is a further reference to a Moabite city[22]; in conjunction with the psalm in xxiv. 8f. this would explain the later insertion of the Moab-saying. Such a distinction between the cities mentioned in ch. xxv and xxvi is also suggested by the fact that in the second psalm a city comparable to Jerusalem is obviously meant, as in xxvi. 1b. It seems to me doubtful, therefore, to supplement the statements of either psalm about the city by the statements of the other psalm. What binds the two psalms together in substance is faith in Yahweh, confirmed by the destruction of the existing city. It is this that seems to have occasioned the secondary insertion of the

[20] On *mbṣr* cf. *beṣurah* in xxv. 2; on *mśgb* cf. *niśgabah* in xxvi. 5; the remainder of xxv. 12 is based on xxvi. 5.
[21] Thus, Eissfeldt (p. 327) adduces Isa. xxxivf., for example, as parallel.
[22] Suggested by Eissfeldt and also discussed by Mulder (pp. 90f.), who thinks of Dibon.

two independent psalms, which are undoubtedly older than the eschatological narrative; the other common element, however, namely the fact that both psalms deal with a ravaged city, requires a brief explanation in what follows.

Jerusalem or Zion is mentioned only twice by name in our apocalypse, firstly in xxiv. 23, which *bahar hazzeh* in xxv. 6 should follow —at present the narrative is interrupted by the hymn of thanksgiving inserted in xxv. 1–5—and secondly in xxv. 10a (*bahar hazzeh*); in both cases the reference to Zion is not in doubt. It has often been observed in expositions of Isa. xxiv–xxvii that it is taken for granted that the group addressed by the apocalypse will remain unscathed by the judgement and that there is also tacit agreement that the scene of Yahweh's epiphany and the great banquet of the nations is the spot that will be exempted from the destruction. It is easy to understand, therefore, that at that point in the course of the eschatological narrative when mention is made of this place of deliverance—it should be noted that it is the place where those being addressed are also to be found—the particular importance of the place has been subsequently underlined by an independent psalm. Since Zion and Jerusalem are referred to by name in xxiv. 23, all that was needed in xxv. 1–5 was a psalm praising Yahweh for appearing at the aforesaid place and proving himself the destroyer of a powerful city and an even more effective refuge[23]; in xxvi. 1–6, on the other hand, it was thought necessary to emphasize his relationship with Jerusalem and the city's strength because previously in xxv. 10a (after the excision of the Moab saying) only 'this mountain' had been referred to. At any rate, there are obviously two independent psalms, probably of older date, derived from other contexts which we can no longer determine, and they have been inserted in the eschatological narrative at a subsequent date in order to give due emphasis to the place that will furnish the scene of deliverance when the world is judged. What was regarded as self-evident within the eschatological narrative could also be given special emphasis by repetition in this way. Perhaps we may take a further step in the interpretation of these psalms. It is quite possible that there is a secondary 'liturgical' purpose linked with the insertion of the two psalms. In the framework of 1 Isaiah (Isa. i–xxxix) the chapters we have been discussing are unique, and their origin cannot be explained in the same way as

---

[23] xxv. 4–5 has been heavily glossed, obviously to provide a smoother transition to xxv. 6; an eschatological passage like that in Isa. iv. 3–6 may have played some part in this.

that of the preceding oracles against foreign nations. The 'Isaiah-Apocalypse' is concerned to corroborate the eschatological hope that was described in the introductory chapters. Such pastoral corroboration must have been necessary from time to time within the eschatological groups, since there would be no shortage of freshly emerging doubts and temptations. Hence, there is nothing to preclude this eschatological 'hand-book' having been improved by a liturgical 'layer' to make it serve a further use. But whatever may be decided about the further history of this eschatological prayer-book, the two psalms in xxv. 1 and xxvi. 1 may be left out of account insofar as they are independent, secondary insertions. They need not be referred to in interpreting the eschatological narrative, which forms the central portion of these chapters.

If the main part of the 'Isaiah-Apocalypse' is to be sought in ch. xxiv–xxvi in the form of different and quite independent eschatological traditions, which have been arranged to form a single narrative, expanded by secondary insertions, particularly in the psalms in xxv. 1f. and xxvi. 1f. and in the short saying about Moab in xxv. 10b–11 or 12, and if the admonition in xxvi. 20f. is to be taken as a conclusion, then the separate parts of ch. xxvii can only be supplementary. They are of very varied character, but it may be asked whether they do not share an almost identical theme. The separate passages are marked by an introductory *bayyom hahu'* (xxvii. 1; xxvii. 2; xxvii. 12 and 13; in xxvii. 6 also a slight change would restore a similar formula) more often than in the previous chapters; only once in ch. xxiv–xxvi does this phrase form part of an originally independent tradition, namely in xxiv. 21, for in xxv. 9 and xxvi. 1 the expression is a verbose addition, serving only as superscription and introduction. But throughout ch. xxvii the formula has eschatological significance[24]; only in xxvii. 2 at the beginning of the vineyard song is there no eschatological significance, since the psalm has a contemporary situation in mind (so Lindblom, p. 54 etc.); an explanation for the unsuitable insertion of the phrase may perhaps be found at the end of the psalm in xxvii. 6, which can be linked with the vineyard song by means of the phrase *bayyamim habba'im* which should be restored in v. 6. In that case we are faced with three distinctly eschatological sections: xxvii. 1, the conflict of Yahweh with enemies who are figuratively likened to mythical beasts;

---

[24] On the eschatological significance of this phrase cf. P. A. Munch, 'The Expression bajjóm hahū, is it an Eschatological Terminus Technicus?' *ANVAO* II, no. 2 (1936).

xxvii. 12 and 13, the hopes of territorial restoration—in xxvii. 12 for the smaller area bounded by the ideal borders of the former Davidic Empire (from the river Euphrates to the Brook of Egypt, cf. 1 Kings v. 1), in xxvii. 13 for the larger area which obviously has in mind the gathering of the Diaspora which will worship in Jerusalem on the holy mountain. This could, in fact, be an independent eschatological account, a parallel to ch. xxiv–xxvi, as Rudolph assumes, although he includes xxvi. 20f. with ch. xxvii. This is not entirely satisfactory; the parallel passage begins in xxvii. 1 with the conflict of Yahweh, resulting in the restoration of Israel, as pictured in xxvii. 12f. Compared with the first eschatological survey in ch. xxiv–xxvi the complex of ideas in ch. xxvii might claim to be substantially older; they are paralleled in the eschatological sections of some of the prophetic books and there may be a reference to a compilation of similar sayings in Isa. xi. 11f.

We are compelled to ask, however, whether any special reason can be given for the addition of this independent eschatological passage. It would be quite easy to think of the passage having been added because the act of gathering together the people of Yahweh in ch. xxiv–xxvi was not adequately described. This explanation would be convincing, if it concerned only vv. 1, 12–13 of ch. xxvii. But what, then, of the intervening verses in xxvii. 2–11? The section xxvii. 2–4 relates the vineyard song not to judgement but to the approaching salvation, although it is undoubtedly based on Isa. v. 1f.[25] Failing other solutions, the significance of this independent psalm in the context of the chapter as a whole may be understood in terms of its synchronism; while Yahweh wages war with his opponents (xxvii. 1), his simultaneous care for his vineyard remains evident; he no longer cherishes any anger against it. In connection with xxvii. 1 'thorns and thistles' will then have to be understood as a reference to Yahweh's enemies, against whom he is proceeding—with warlike intent, it is stressed, in an unnecessary gloss. But the link with xxvii. 1 should probably not be made too tight. The clause in xxvii. 4b ('would that I had thorns and thistles . . .'), referring to external enemies, could be taken for granted after xxvii. 1, without overlooking that the vineyard is an independent unit employing its own ideas. In view of the following verse 5 ('. . . or let them lay hold of my protection and make peace with me . . .') Duhm (p. 165) had already considered the possibility of interpreting the thorns and thistles as

---

[25] For the textual difficulties at the beginning of the psalm reference should be made to Lindblom (pp. 54f.).

opponents of the Jewish theocracy, in which case the eschatological prospect in xxvii. 6 would refer to internal peace. In connection with the hope of restoration for ancient Israel (Davidic—xxvii. 12) which is emphasized throughout ch. xxvii, and in view of the parallels in Isa. xi. 11f. mentioned above, I suspect that the terms Jacob and Israel in xxvii. 6 have a special meaning, i.e., they refer to the inclusion of the former Northern kingdom. The names Jacob and Israel neither favour this nor tell against it. Their use in the later additions to the prophetic writings is so varied as to provide no sufficient criterion for deciding. But if they did refer to the Northern kingdom the opposition in xxvii. 4b and 5 would be equally understandable as an internal opposition, even if not in Duhm's sense, and above all it would be easy to understand vv. 7 and 8 from the fate of the former Northern kingdom and its deported oppressor, Assyria. I follow the translation suggested by Rudolph (p. 8) with corresponding emendations: 'Has it (meaning the Northern kingdom) been smitten like the one that smote it (meaning Assyria), or slain like its slayers, for it was punished with exile and removed by thy fierce blast in the day of the east wind?' These are brief reminiscences of Ephraim's fate, evoked by the view that the previous tribes of the North, their kinsmen, also belong to Yahweh's vineyard, if they submit—xxvii. 5 could be paraphrased in this way—to the jurisdiction of Jerusalem. This also gives a new meaning to the statement in xxvii. 9, which is quite inappropriate as it stands. To make peace with Yahweh means to remove the cultic aberrations of the paganized population of the old Northern kingdom; in positive terms this means subjection to the only legitimate cult, namely that of the Jerusalem community. We should have to seek the historical situation in the tensions between Jerusalem and the 'foolish people of Shechem' which are referred to in the Books of Ezra and Nehemiah. But the hopes expressed in ch. xxvii were probably not published by exclusively Jerusalemite circles, such as were represented by Nehemiah, for instance, but by people who were convinced of Jerusalem's cultic legitimacy and who had, nevertheless, in obedience to numerous passages of prophetic tradition, not lost faith in a restoration of ancient Israel as it had once appeared in the time of David. They obviously felt that the differences which existed between the two parts of the former Israel were not the last word.

It cannot be denied that such a view harmonizes well with the dominant expectations in ch. xxvii regarding a restoration of Israel. This is also true of the final section of the chapter to be treated,

F

namely vv. 10 and 11, although it is impossible to avoid emending the text at this point. Disregarding xxvii. 10aα ('for the fortified city is solitary') initially, we have before us a description, portraying briefly the desolation of a region or city which has been subject to divine judgement, and possessing remote parallels in Isa. xiii and xiv, for instance. The passage cannot be described as felicitous; nor do the women gathering brushwood exactly succeed in improving the verse. Yet the final clause of xxvii. 11 tells in favour of the interpretation suggested above: the inhabitants of the desolate country are called a people without discernment, upon whom their creator will not have mercy. This remark does not really fit the surviving inhabitants of the ravaged city mentioned in the hymns of thanksgiving. This suggests, therefore, that we should consider them to be people who stand in a special relationship to their creator, which can only be Yahweh. Duhm felt this difficulty and therefore thought of the inhabitants of Jerusalem in xxvii. 11; his reason, however, that only 'Jews (not Samaritans) could be censured for having no insight' (p. 167), is hardly true for the late date to which he assigns these verses. At any rate, Sir. 1. 25f. says, 'For two nations I feel contempt, and the third is no nation; those who dwell on Mt. Seir (Edom) and the Philistines and the foolish people who dwell in Shechem!' It is true that Isa. xxvii. 11 also does not expect very much from the inhabitants of the old Northern kingdom, whose cultic aberrations are condemned in xxvii. 9; but it does expect that the restoration of what was once created by Yahweh and has been corroborated afresh by the mouth of the prophet lies within the bounds of Yahweh's possibility.

We cannot simply bypass xxvii. 10aα, however. Once again the ghost of the accursed fortified city haunts the verse and clouds the view; in fact, this city, which plays such a large part in the two hymns of thanksgiving, seems to be the chief enemy that is constantly impeding the interpretation of our apocalypse. Granted that without xxvii. 10aα the transition from xxvii. 9 to xxvii. 10aβ is difficult, I can only assume that something stood here which was found to be unintelligible and was replaced by borrowing from the first part of the apocalypse. Perhaps Duhm was not so ill-advised after all when he tried to link the fortified city in the apocalypse with Samaria, even though his assumption that it referred to the destruction of Samaria under John Hyrcanus can hardly be right. Whatever may be the case with this brief sentence in xxvii. 10aα—whether it is a secondary gloss, trying to make up for something that has been lost but only adding to the confusion by mistaken borrowing, or whether the city conceals a reference to life and activity in Shechem or Samaria together with reminiscences of the situation after the destruction caused by the Assyrians, who are naturally thought of from the Jewish point of view—there is no doubt in my mind that the separate units of ch. xxvii are held together by a specific theme, namely the re-unification of the two separated parts that once made up Israel, subject, of course, to the clear pre-eminence of Jerusalem. From this point of view we can confidently regard ch. xxvii as an addition which does not contribute very much to the interpretation of the eschatological narrative in ch. xxiv–xxvi. It is a collection of certain 'eschatologoumena', added at a later date, dedicated to the theme 're-unification', and appended as a supplement. It was felt to be necessary because the main eschatological section pays hardly any attention to this very important viewpoint of eschatological doctrine, either because it is taken for granted or because other aims are at work in the first chapters, which seek to treat the eschatological theme in a more comprehensive fashion and on the basis of fundamental considerations. It is quite probable, therefore, that the views which come to light in ch. xxvii belong to an earlier period. A brief summary of our examination so far must now be appended.

We have to reckon with two independent parts in the Isaiah-Apocalypse, both of which belong together because they display an eschatological viewpoint, although what we call 'eschatological' cannot be completely harmonized in the two parts. The first and more extensive part deals with the *eschaton* more fundamentally, insofar as the end of the world and the resultant consequences are actually described, whereas the shorter section that was added at a later date deals with an end that will usher in a definitive form of the ancient people of God, without considering whether history itself —irrespective of detail—will continue beyond this point or not. The first part consists of a description, into which previously independent units have sometimes been inserted and dovetailed, probably for purposes of illustration, and to which independent units have some-times just been added unaltered. It begins with a description of the eschatological judgement on the whole of mankind (xxiv. 1–6), a judgement that does not stop short at urban civilization (xxiv. 7–13); it rejects premature rejoicing which sees the great turning-point already arriving in preliminary events which are not yet eschatological; and it sharpens the eschatological perspective for this reason (xxiv. 14–20). This could be the point to begin searching for the origins, now no longer visible, of our eschatological passage. The obscurities may have arisen within the eschatological groups; there must have been members in their ranks who saw the great revolution presaged in events which were certainly important but which were not felt by other representatives of this eschatological outlook to be eschatological, and who broke out in premature rejoicing, a reference perhaps to those belonging to the Jewish Diaspora. In contrast, the eschatological narrative in what was presumably its initial form emphasizes the calamitousness and cosmic dimensions of the eschatological events. At the same time or somewhat later, but at any rate for different reasons, this eschatological narrative is given shape with the help of independent traditions (xxiv. 21–23 and xxv. 6–8); it describes the epiphany of Yahweh on Zion after the disarmament of the enemy and ends with the great universal banquet of the nations at the place of the epiphany. The answer of the present inhabitants of Zion who subscribe to such a belief consists of an expression of trust that the protective hand of the judge of the world will rest on Zion (xxv. 9–10a) and passes into a reflection which enables us to infer why such a continuation of the eschatological survey was required (xxvi. 7f.). The traditional contrast of righteous and godless is used, but it is clear that this contrast has been given a contemporary meaning; the righteous are those who accept the eschatological insight revealed in the preceding description, namely the fact that history is hastening to its end, while the godless are included among the enemies of Yahweh because they refuse to acknowledge this same insight (xxvi. 7–11). This obviously refers to an internal (Jewish) division between a section of the Jewish community that has an eschatological outlook and a section that is not interested in the eschatological faith, although specific characteristics which would facilitate a more precise determination of the two groups cannot be given. We recollect what was said in the previous chapter of the present study about the eschatologically disinterested view which emerged in the historical work of the Chronicler, a view which probably reflects the position of the ruling classes and especially the priests, and it is our opinion that this same division is to be found again in the Isaiah-Apocalypse. The striking severity of the division may be explained by the fact that in the Jewish community the eschatological faith is not permitted to die out but must be kept alive because the eschatological groups found it to be necessary. A further passage (xxvi. 12–19), on the other hand, is aimed at these selfsame eschatologically-minded groups, and here it is clearly a case of overcoming doubt and temptation in their own ranks; the decisive eschatologoumenon, referred to in a divine oracle as a sign of the end, is the resurrection (xxvi. 19), personal confirmation, so to speak, in contrast to the public eschatological banquet of rejoicing in xxv. 6–8, for those who are willing to remain loyal to their eschatological faith in spite of temptations. An admonition of the speaker—one could call him a prophet if one understands by that the contemporary interpreter of prophetic traditions—concludes the whole passage in xxvi. 20f.

Secondary insertions in the form of hymns of thanksgiving (xxv. 1–5; xxvi. 1–6)—undoubtedly stemming from an earlier period and worked in either to emphasize Mount Zion, which has been mentioned from time to time, or for liturgical reasons, because similar temptations, such as the doubts expressed in xxvi. 7f., necessitated a continuing use of the passage—together with a saying about Moab (xxv, 10b–12), the historical occasion of which cannot be more closely determined, although it is to be dated later than the hymns of thanksgiving, do not contribute a great deal to the understanding of this part of the Isaiah-Apocalypse.

No chronology can be suggested for the apocalypse except within rough outlines. Marked characteristics of later apocalyptic, such as the sharp distinction between the present and the future age, are still foreign to the Isaiah-Apocalypse. But the judgement of the world is already understood as a universal-cosmic event; and the resurrection of the dead, a sign of the eschatological revolution for those who hold fast to this faith, brings our passage even nearer to the Book of Daniel.[26] Hence, the century of Ptolemaic rule may be suggested as the general period and more specifically the latter part of this period, when the beginning of the rule of Antiochus the Great and the consequent political contest for Palestine between the Seleucids and the Ptolemies probably caused fairly serious unrest. Behind the document we should probably assume there were certain groups of the Jewish community in Palestine, who knew they were fairly deeply divorced from the official line within the community because of their eschatological convictions.

The second part of the apocalypse, which is limited to ch. xxvii, is much older. It seems to recommend the re-unification of Israel within the territory of the former Davidic empire; it is aware of the

---

[26] For the characteristics of a transitional period cf. the distinction of actualizing and dualistic eschatology suggested by Vriezen ('Prophecy and Eschatology', *VT* 3 (1953), pp. 227f.).

cultic aberrations and the lack of discernment on the part of the pagan population of the earlier Northern kingdom, but does not give up hope of a reconciliation brought about by Yahweh. The Samaritan schism seems to be still in the future, so far as it is possible to draw any valid general conclusion from independent units of different periods. It may perhaps be assumed that definite hopes of restoration, such as were alive in the early Persian period, had not completely died out in some verses at least. We are brought perhaps to the times of tension between Jerusalem and Shechem in the decades before and perhaps also after the activity of Ezra and Nehemiah, when we should already be able to perceive a cleavage within the population of Jerusalem; not everybody, certainly not all the eschatological groups, shared the exclusive view evident in the proceedings of Nehemiah. The secondary addition of this chapter to the Isaiah-Apocalypse is to be understood as a supplement. Ever since the time of the monarchy that was now passing away, the re-unification of ancient Israel belonged to the hopes which had not yet died out; later it became an important point in eschatological doctrine and was not forgotten by those groups in whose midst ch. xxiv–xxvii were probably formed.

2. 'TRITO-ZECHARIAH' (Zech. xii–xiv)

Our more limited survey of the last three chapters of the Book of Zechariah presents far more difficulties than the Isaiah-Apocalypse. In view of the alarming variety and difference of opinions it is almost unnecessary to add a further interpretation which could only repeat or modify one of the possibilities already considered. Even the question of partitioning ch. ix–xiv, which are distinct from Proto-Zechariah (Zech. i–viii), is not undisputed, since Stade[27] recommended the derivation of these chapters from the hand of an author whom he wished to date between 300 and 280 B.C., thus challenging frequently held opinions, such as that ch. ix–xi contain pre-exilic portions. Marti[28] followed Stade's view regarding the unity of ch. ix–xiv, but wished to date the author more than a hundred years later, i.e., about 160 B.C. and assigned him to a point midway between the Maccabeans and the *Hasidim*. But this did not silence the assumption that the chapters were the work of several

---

[27] B. Stade, 'Deuterozacharja', *ZAW* (1881), pp. 1–96; (1882), pp. 151–72, and pp. 275–209.

[28] K. Marti, *Dodekapropheton*, KHC 13 (1904).

authors nor the assumption that a pre-exilic document had been revised and expanded in the Greek period. As a comparative indication of how little we can rely on fixed conclusions we may instance the vacillation of Sellin, who at first accepted a post-exilic origin only for ch. xiv, deriving ch. ix–xi from the time of Isaiah and ch. xiif. from the time of Jeremiah, but later argued for the origin of ch. ix–xiii in the long period between the activity of Ezra-Nehemiah and the Maccabees, with ch. xiv as an independent addition; finally (in the last edition of his commentary[29]) he considered it was derived from groups of *Hasidim*, somewhat later, in fact, than Daniel. But this very late dating was not uncontested. Nowack,[30] maintaining the unity of ch. ix–xiii, arrived at a date of origin similar to that previously assumed by Stade (300–280 B.C.), dating ch. xiv some years later, while Horst[31] not only regarded it more appropriate to locate ch. ix–xi towards the end of the Persian period but also thought it possible to take into account the introduction of older material (from the period 740–730 B.C.); ch. xii–xiv, however, were to be regarded as a separate unit and assigned to the third century B.C. Mitchell[32] had already considered the possibility that ix 1–10 should be regarded as an appendix to ch. i–viii, written soon after the battle of Issus (333) and expanded during the third century B.C. to include the years after the battle of Raphia (217); similarly, Elliger[33] thought the beginning of ch. ix could be connected with the campaign of Alexander the Great into Syria and Phoenicia, so that the main parts of ch. ix–xi, which make constant reference to historical situations, stem from approximately the same period of the early Hellenistic age, whereas ch. xiif. and xiv, which stand out from ch. ix–xi by reason of their developed eschatology and more pronounced literary character, probably belong to the Ptolemaic period; there is no need, however, to come down into the Maccabean period.

If we take up Elliger's observation, referred to above, that a marked eschatological character is more evident for ch. xii–xiv, and supplement it by reference to Eissfeldt's[34] remark that there are no traces in these chapters that point to a pre-exilic period of origin, then

---

[29] E. Sellin, *Das Zwölfprophetenbuch*, KAT XII 2 (1930).
[30] W. Nowack, *Die Kleinen Propheten*, HK III no. 4 (1922³).
[31] Th. H. Robinson and F. Horst, *Die zwölf kleinen Propheten*, HAT I no. 14 (1954²).
[32] H. G. Mitchell, *Haggai, Zechariah*, ICC (1912).
[33] K. Elliger, *Das Buch der zwölf kleinen Propheten*, ATD 25 (1950). A detailed analysis of Zech. ix–xiv has just been published: P. Lamarche, *Zacharie IX–XIV. Structure littéraire et Messianisme*, EB (1961).
[34] O. Eissfeldt, *The Old Testament: an Introduction*, p. 439.

this favours the restriction of our examination to ch. xii–xiv, although this must be prefaced by a brief survey of ch. ix–xi.

Ch. ix begins with a series of sayings against Aramaic, Phoenician and Philistinian states and cities, which may be included in the narrower compass of Syria and Palestine. The form and structure of the section is characterized by the succession of prophetic (ix. 1–6a) and divine speech (ix. 6b–8). These verses, as Horst recently suggested again, may consist entirely of pre-exilic traditions, which were transformed and expanded when they took on contemporary significance again as a result of recent political developments. It is natural to think of the political confusion in connection with the campaign of Alexander. Be that as it may, after 350 B.C. Persia made several further attempts under Artaxerxes III to conquer Egypt and connect it more firmly to the Persian Empire. The failure of the first attempt was followed by revolts in Cyprus, Syria and Phoenicia. The undertaking did not succeed until 343/2 when the native king Nektanebos fled to Nubia.[35] The disturbances associated with these military operations may, in fact, supply the contemporary background for ix. 1–8 shortly before this. The continuation in ix. 11–17 deals with the return of the prisoners in a somewhat indefinite form (e.g. it is not stated where the prisoners are returning from) and also with the political struggle for freedom, undertaken jointly by Judah and Ephraim under Yahweh's leadership; the section is obviously intended to be taken as a consequence of the message declared in ix. 1–8, even if it derives from another author. Predominant in the description of the future that is to be found in this section, which offers further evidence of the connection of divine utterance and prophetic utterance, is the view of the former Davidic Empire, from which, however, the land east of Jordan has been completely excluded. In addition there is a definitely secondary continuation in x. 3–12, which is much more interested in the return of the Diaspora when dealing with a restoration of the ancient people of God; consequently, in comparison with ix. 1–8, it extends the horizon considerably and threatens the former great powers of Assyria and Egypt, perhaps in the modern dress of Seleucid and Ptolemaic rule, with disarmament and destruction. The mention of Gilead (x. 10), the ancient granary of the land east of Jordan, seems to be a brief addition to complete ix. 11–17. The passage is linked with the previous section by its military character, even if the disarmament of the great powers that is envisaged bears a stronger

[35] U. Kahrstedt, *Geschichte des griechisch-römischen Altertums* (1948), pp. 82, 84.

eschatological stamp. The form is again marked by the alternation
of prophetic and divine utterance. If the first three verses of ch. xi
which were obviously thought of as rounding off what has preceded,
are included, then we can speak of the comparative compactness of
the narrative, which is recounted in several stages; its archaisms and
great respect for human help proclaim the restoration of ancient
Israel, the disarmament of the enemy in both narrower and wider
compass and the return home of the Diaspora, in all of which it has
undoubtedly undergone both suitable (ix. 9f.) and unsuitable (x. 1f.)
insertions. It is striking that Jerusalem plays no part in all this;
apart from the insertion ix. 9f. Zion³⁶ is mentioned only in ix. 13,
where it has no special significance alongside Judah and Ephraim,
but may be understood from the perspective of the former Davidic
Empire. Since the chapters which interest us, ch. xii–xiv, deal
almost exclusively with Jerusalem, the combination of these chapters
in this way may have had definite significance, although there was
no original connection between ch. xii f. and the series discussed
above (ix. 1–8; 11–17; x. 3–12). This is also true of the narrative
in xi. 4–17, which is reminiscent of a prophetic symbolic act and
can scarcely be regarded as the original continuation of the above
series; in fact, it surveys certain historical events in dress which
already has the appearance of apocalyptic. A detailed exposition of
each separate point cannot be undertaken here and reference must
be made to the interpretations suggested in the commentaries. It
seems as if historical events that were quite familiar to the group,
for whom this allegorical survey was written, may have given rise
to questions and are being interpreted as 'mysteries'. Interpretation
is also rendered more difficult for us because the allegory is clearly
fragmentary in its present form; nor can it be improved by the
insertion of the passage xiii. 7–9, as has been customary since Ewald.
There is a great deal of evidence that the breaking of the two staves
(i.e., in the dissolution of the covenant between Yahweh and the
nations and in the breaking of the bond of brotherhood between
Judah and Ephraim) contains a reference to events which are connected with the Macedonian expedition against the Persian Empire
and also with the Samaritan schism, which can be fitted into roughly
the same period.³⁷ The significance of xi. 4–17, a most striking
section when seen in its context, seems to lie in the fact that in con-

---

³⁶ But cf. the suggested omission of *sion* in BH on metrical grounds; the emendation suggested by Marti in ix. 12aα (*wᵉšābû lāk bat̄-ṣiôn* instead of *šûbû lᵉbiṣṣārôn*)
does not commend itself to me.

³⁷ Cf. Horst, p. 253 and Elliger, pp. 153f.

trast to previous hopes of restoration, which presuppose the restoration of Israel as their unquestioned goal, a stricter delineation of the eschatological aspect was regarded as necessary. Thus, in comparison with attempts at justification on the part of the Jewish community in connection with the Samaritan schism it was felt to be far more important to interpret these events eschatologically; renewed pressure from Yahweh was to be traced behind the disturbances in the international world and behind the conflicts in 'God's own land', a pressure that would not introduce the restoration painlessly, however, but would involve the tribulations of a painful judgement. Because ch. xii–xiv are concerned particularly with this greater severity, the shepherd allegory was, in fact, a good transition from the traditional eschatology predominant in ix. 1–xi. 13 to a new type of understanding of Yahweh's eschatological activity, evident in certain elements of ch. xii–xiv.

Normally the first longer unit in the last three chapters of the Book of Zechariah is taken to stretch as far as xiii. 6 (inclusive); the brief sword-saying in xiii. 7–9 is excised, since it is linked with the shepherd allegory in xi. 4–17, and ch. xiv is regarded as an independent unit, which should be dated somewhat later. Within the first large unit—the superscription in xii. 1 may be ignored, since it clearly applies to all three chapters—we notice in the first half a sequence of separate sayings, which are separated from each other by the phrase 'on that day', while in the second half of xii. 11–14 or from xii. 9–14 onwards, since the announcement made in xii. 11–14 requires an introduction, a greater compactness is evident; a similar judgement may be made about xiii. 1–6, insofar as the theme announced in xiii. 1 is developed along several lines. In view of this formal unevenness between the two halves of xii. 1–xiii. 6 it may be assumed that the chief stress is on the second half, which manifests greater compactness. But, in that case, why did it need such a detailed introduction, comprising almost half the whole passage and referring to things which play no further part in the second half? In the second half we are concerned exclusively with the house of David and the inhabitants of Jerusalem, whereas in the first half it is Judah, the tents and clans[38] of Judah, that are spoken of as important. The fact that xii. 1–8 is filled with additions is widely noted in the commentaries; as might be expected, it is only the extent of what is to be excised as a gloss that is subject to uncertainty. Here Elliger (ATD, p. 158), on the basis of the verses and

[38] This should be read in xii. 5 and 6 instead of 'chiefs of Judah'.

parts of verses that he rejects (xii. 2b, 3b, 4bα, 6a, 7f.), has pointed out a compact sequence of thought, 'which is apparently formulated with an eye to xii. 2–6, which deals only with Jerusalem, and aims to make good the omission of the provinces'. Only xii. 5 (the astonishing affirmation of the people of Judah that the inhabitants of Jerusalem trust in Yahweh alone for their strength) and xii. 6b (Jerusalem will remain in its present position) should be included in the basic document according to Elliger; in the case of xii. 1–8 this means only vv. 2a, 3a, 4abβ, 5, 6b. If we accept Elliger's suggestion, however, it may be questioned whether xii. 6b really does form the conclusion of the original piece, as Elliger assumes, or whether we should not also consider the excision of vv. 5 and 6b from the original document. The remaining section, xii. 2–4, to be reduced by the omission of several glosses (more precisely xii. 2a, 3a, 4abβ), seems to be equally disturbed by the glosses that have been inserted. The succession of the two different types of pictures, a cup of reeling and a heavy stone, may remain without cavil; but, since the second picture (of a heavy stone) has an explanation attached, something similar might also be expected for the first picture (of the cup of reeling), especially since on other occasions the use of the picture of a cup of reeling is linked with an explanation.[39] It should be considered, therefore, whether xii. 4a ('I will strike every horse with panic and their riders with madness . . .') which now appears as an independent saying, was not originally regarded as interpreting xii. 2a; it should also be asked whether xii. 4bβ ('and I will strike every horse of the peoples with blindness') was not first occasioned by the gloss xii. 4bα ('but upon Judah I will open my eyes'); these may be secondary questions, however. Altogether the now extensive eschatological theme of an attack on Jerusalem by the nations would have been only a brief introduction originally, acting as a chronological introduction and transition to xii. 9f, the point which obviously occupies the centre of the whole passage: the contemporary change of heart by the Jerusalemites. Thus, the somewhat unusual *'abakkeš* in xii. 9 may be understood in this way ('on that day I will seek to destroy all the nations that come against Jerusalem'): xii. 9 presupposes only a brief introductory phrase before passing—in the midst of Yahweh's dealings with the hostile army of the various nations—to the things which are described within Jerusalem from xii. 10 onwards.

This description is full of riddles. It concerns a change of purpose

[39] Thus e.g. Jer. xxv. 15f.; li. 39; Obad. 16; Ps. lxxv. 9.

wrought by Yahweh in the house of David and the population of Jerusalem, which expresses itself in a large funeral for an unnamed person, of whose death the mourners are not entirely innocent. The description of this mourning is developed graphically in two directions; firstly, in xii. 10b and 11 it is compared with the mourning for the only or first-born son, then in xii. 11 this is expanded with a new comparison, namely the mourning rites for Hadad-Rimmon in the Megiddo plain. No great significance should be attributed to the details of the second comparison. It is a reference to the customary cultic mourning for the dying and rising god among the Canaanites, which had already been transferred as a result of syncretism to the weather-god Hadad, who in turn had become linked with an Aramaic deity Rimmon (Ramman); it is easy to see, therefore, that from the point of view of Jerusalem the Megiddo plain could stand for the nearest part of the country to where this cult was practised.[40] Further, to illustrate the intensity of the lament reference is made to the fact that the whole country participated; the population is divided into men and women and participation in the mourning is in accord with this division; in xii. 12f. the most eminent families are named.

Naturally in the first instance questions revolve round the mysterious figure of the one who has been pierced, who by virtue of being nameless seems to stand in some relationship to the threatening position of Jerusalem, but who in view of the change of heart by the people of Jerusalem also seems to stand in some relationship to the prevention of this distress. But the identification of this personality with a figure familiar to us from Israelite-Jewish history, a task made more difficult by textual corruption,[41] has little hope of success, whether we come down as far as the Maccabean period and are thus able to offer concrete suggestions—for the simple reason that

[40] So Horst, p. 256; similarly Sellin, pp. 575f., whereas Junker (*HSAT, Die zwölf kleinen Propheten* VIII 3 no. 2 (1938), p. 180) follows the older interpretation which, following a remark in Hieronymus, regarded Hadadrimmon as a place near Megiddo and thought of the lament as being for King Josiah who was killed at Megiddo (2 Kings xxiii. 29f.), a lament which survived for a long time amongst the people according to 2 Chron. xxxv. 25. Junker does, however, mention the interpretation suggested by van Hoonacker, namely that it concerns a place in the tribe of Benjamin, the name of which has been distorted (*hărimmōn 'ašer bᵉmigrōn*, 1 Sam. xiv. 2); it may have played a part in the expedition to punish the tribe of Benjamin (Judges xxf.) in connection with a rock *hărimmōn* (Judges xx. 45, 47), and it may also have been connected with a rite of mourning by the whole people (Judges xxi. 2f.).

[41] The MT reads *'ēlay 'et*; the usual emendation to *'eley 'et* may be retained since the suffix of the first person singular in *'elay* could only refer to Yahweh and this is impossible. Wellhausen's suggestion that we should see in the last three consonants of *'ly't* the mutilated name of the pierced figure only underlines our difficulty.

we know more about this period than about the previous century (so Marti, Sellin etc.), or whether it be a figure of the past (Josiah, Jeremiah, Zerubbabel), in which case its relationship to the events now taking place must be largely a matter of inference. Thus, the only other solution is to turn to Isa. liii and give consideration to a transformation of the theme of the suffering servant of God in connection with a martyr-type figure, the details of which are not known to us. It does not take us any further if we link the one who has been pierced with a figure of the shepherd-allegory in xi. 4f., because the contemporary historical events presupposed there are equally obscure to us. The names of what are obviously the four most eminent families who participate in the mourning also provide plenty of riddles. The reference to the house of David, which—apart from additions in xii. 1–8—we have met in xii. 10 along with the population of Jerusalem, can hardly be explained from the pre-exilic situation, because in that case one would have expected the king to be named; nor can it be understood in the general sense of 'rule' with no genealogical relationship to the family of David, but it must probably be connected with a period in which the family of David (*gens davidica*) held a position in the Jewish community corresponding to their traditional authority. This brings us to the Persian period at the earliest, when members of the family of David are said to occupy a leading position, if the Shemaiah ben Shecaniah mentioned in Neh. iii. 29 is identical with a son of David of the same name in 1 Chron. iii. 22 and—some decades later—a son of David, Hanani (1 Chron. iii. 24), may be identified with the (H)Anani who is mentioned in the Elephantine Papyri as being at Jerusalem between 410 and 405. If we adopt the usual explanation which regards the tribe of Nathan, the son of David (according to 2 Sam. v. 14; 1 Chron. iii. 5), as a branch of the family tree of David, while Levi and Shimei refer to a collection of priestly groups, in which Shimei (a grandson of Levi, Num. iii. 17f; 1 Chron. vi. 26) would represent a branch of the tree like Nathan within the *gens davidica*, then perhaps we may see in what may be a deliberately incomplete enumeration a phrase that was coined for a particular occasion but then came to be used for other similar occasions.

One has the impression that there is a definite historical event behind this mysterious description; but we know too little of Jewish history between Ezra/Nehemiah and the Maccabean period to be able to say anything definite. One of these few recorded events during the last century of Persian rule was the murder by the High Priest

Johannes of his brother Jesus in the Temple precinct, which is described by Josephus (Ant. xi. 7.1) with great indignation as an outrage without precedent among Greeks or barbarians. In view of the atonement demanded by the Persian governor Bagoas from the Jewish community for the next seven years, it is understandable that this event imprinted itself on the memory, especially since there was at that time—probably for the first time in the history of the post-exilic Temple—a 'profanation' of the Temple. Bagoas entered the Temple without meeting active resistance because the Jews had nothing to set against his argument that he felt he was cleaner and worthier than the High Priest who had profaned the Temple by murder. This double profanation was certainly expiated by corresponding days of repentance, even if we have no knowledge of the High Priest being dismissed from office. The High Priest Johanan held office between 411–408,[42] i.e., about the same time that the Davidic Hanani occupied a distinguished position (perhaps as president of the council) within the Jewish community according to the evidence of the Elephantine texts. Is it erroneous to connect Zech. xii. 10f. with this event, which certainly led to a great ceremony of public repentance in which the 'house of David' (represented by Hanani standing at the head of the secular dignitaries) took part along with the priesthood, which—perhaps significantly—does not include any specific mention of the High Priest? In that case, however, the 'gazing on the pierced one' would refer less to the person of the one who has been killed than to the consequences of the Temple being profaned through their own fault, an act which would naturally affect the whole theocratic community. We should have to refrain from connecting the person of the pierced one directly with the eschatological event. There is no doubt that the consecutive perfects in xii. 10 in connection with a divine utterance offer considerable difficulties. We should have to understand the utterance as follows: in view of the eschatological attack of the nations Yahweh brings about this change of heart on the part of the Jerusalemites, but the realization of this repentance takes place in the rites prescribed in the cult; i.e., the message in Zech. xii. 10 aims simply to affirm that a great lament is held by all the people at the beginning of the eschatological distress, and this takes place according to the forms that had been customary, and were, in fact, perhaps legally prescribed, since the outrage committed by the High Priest in Jerusalem. In view of the following sections in ch. xiiif. we might

[42] On this cf. K. Galling, ATD 12, pp. 13 f.

infer that our composition in Zech. xii–xiv does not seem content with such a ritual lament. It will be wise, however, to conclude our survey of the rest of the composition first; this will be only a rough outline and will primarily consider the present arrangement of the separate, independent parts.

Thus, the next section xiii. 1–6 is certainly not the direct continuation of ch. xii; it reads like a development of the theme stated in xiii. 1 and illustrated with a number of examples. The theme is connected with ch. xii by the reference to the house of David; it deals with the removal of idols and degenerate prophecy. The suppression of idol worship had always been a live issue in the history of Israel, even if what was understood by idol worship was subject to a certain amount of fluctuation depending on the period. The theocratic community of the post-exilic period laid particular emphasis upon this task, although their efforts were not always attended with obvious success. The remarks about the prophets, who in xiii. 2 are summarily regarded as 'bearers' of the unclean spirit, seem to rest on personal experience, as Elliger (ATD, p. 163) rightly points out. This, then was the way in which contemporary prophecy, no longer important, was regarded within the theocracy, and occasionally an example was made of a prophet, as when a man's own family, either voluntarily or under pressure of public opinion, went against such a 'prophetic' member in its midst, or when such a 'prophetic' figure became the object of general ridicule. The author of the passage under discussion is in full agreement with this judgement and with the elimination of prophecy; he has ceased to expect anything further from contemporary prophets and knows that the prophetic spirit is at work elsewhere as indicated in the present composition. But the distinctive feature of the passage, it seems to me, lies in another direction. However much the author of the present passage—which is not to say that he was responsible for every single strand within it—may have been convinced of the justification of the proceedings against sin and uncleanness, the fact that the attempted suppression of uncleanness, although quite successful in part, will not find its fulfilment until the eschatological revolution and that this is the last word that can be expected about purification and renewal, presumably seems to him to result in too pale a picture of the eschatological Israel. Hence xiii. 6 cannot be the conclusion of a finished composition. What we have regarded as a unity, xi. 2–xiii. 6, itself a combination of several parts, is only the introduction; it requires a continuation, which, again originally independent, is to be found in xiii. 7–9. Whether the brief saying is a unity in itself can be deferred at this stage; for the purpose of our present investigation it will be treated as a whole. A certain unevenness is understandable, since the phraseology is influenced by 'reminiscences' (Duhm) of older prophetic sayings; but this is not sufficient reason for omitting vv. 8–9 completely. Thus for xiii. 7a reference should be made to Ezek. xxi. 21, for xiii. 7b to 1 Kings xxii. 17, while xiii. 8 may refer to Isa. vi. 13 as well as to Ezek. v. 1f., and refinement by fire has prophetic parallels in Isa. i. 25; Jer. vi. 27, 30, ix. 6. Elliger rightly points to the fact that in contrast to the source referred to in xiii. 1, where uncleanness is washed away, purification by fire is to be thought of as more searching, just as the situation of the Last Day (*Endzeit*) altogether is taken more seriously (ATD, p. 167). Hence it will be more accurate to interpret the addition of this independent section not only as an expansion but also as a deliberate sharpening of perspective. This, at any rate, seems to have been the task which the author intended for vv. 7–9 at this point of his composition; originally they probably belonged to other contexts; the generally suggested connection with the shepherd allegory in xi. 4f. seems worth considering, although it is not altogether convincing. The sharpening of perspective is revealed in the fact that Yahweh calls for his sword against his shepherd, who is to be slain and his flock scattered. In 1 Kings xxii where the prophet compares Israel to a flock without a shepherd there is undoubtedly a reference to the king. Here, too, the shepherd is Israel's representative, if not its king, and in the framework of the Jewish theocracy there is nothing to preclude our thinking of the High Priest, who represented the Jewish community before the Persian king—as well as before God; *geber ʿamiti* in xiii. 7 need not signify anything more. It is all the more significant that this earthly pinnacle of the theocracy is overturned by Yahweh himself and not even the insignificant members of the flock, who can, of course, always rejoice in the special care of Yahweh, can count on being spared. In fact, punishment is a consequence of testing, and the consistent application of the prophetic idea of the remnant suggests that an undefined but qualified remnant will represent the eschatological Israel, which Yahweh will call his people (xiii. 9). There is no suggestion that the definition of this tried and tested remnant has been deliberately left undecided. The extremely rigorous actualization of the prophetic idea of the remnant, which once had a special significance for the constitution of the Jewish community, suggests that there was a clear idea which group of people could be identified with this purified remnant. Once again it seems to be those who think and hope eschatologically, men of insight; in contrast to their co-religionists, who also take divine judgements into full consideration but expect the purification in a formal, ritualistic manner without painful intervention and have thus occupied a supposedly secure position in the van of the eschatological decisions, they take up the cause of a painful intensification of the eschatological judgement; they can do this because they possess a living faith that they belong to the tested remnant, the true Israel in the eschatological sense.

It seems clear to me that on such an interpretation xiii. 7–9 occupies a necessary place between the larger unit xii. 2–xiii. 6 and ch. xiv, not in the sense of a 'second course', as Elliger expresses the view he disagrees with, but as an integral part of the total composition. In his commentary (p. 184) Junker tried to understand xiii. 7–9 as 'a shorter parallel to ch. xiv'; according to Junker the section might perhaps be an introduction to ch. xiv, 'anticipating the main contents of the following narrative in a brief synopsis'. But xiii. 7–9 is more than just a parallel; it is the divine announcement of what is depicted in ch. xiv, although the two passages are quite independent; in this connection it may be significant that there is no longer any evidence of Yahweh speaking in the first person in ch. xiv.[43] Thus, briefly anticipating our conclusion, the whole composition of ch. xii–xiv is concerned with the same event. But whereas in xii. 2–xiii. 6 the view is directed to the inner preparation of the theocratic community and the way it confronts the eschatological activity of Yahweh, a preparation which comes to a halt in cultic formalities and preliminaries, with the result, however, that the rigour of Yahweh's eschatological activity in all its severity is all the more visible, ch. xiv ends with the new Jerusalem of the purified remnant, into which Yahweh himself will enter. Before turning to a consideration of the overall interpretation of the composition we must briefly summarize ch. xiv.

Even a hasty reading of this chapter leaves an impression of discord. At first it seems as if one could rely on a certain compactness of narrative. This impression stems partly from the contrast of ch. xiif. and ch. xiv; for in spite of certain decorative and repetitive features ch. xiv, in comparison with ch. xiif., evidences greater purposefulness in pursuit of its theme. But on closer inspection this initial impression is considerably weakened. The deeper reason for

---

[43] Apart from xiv. 2; but on this cf. the following footnote.

G

this discrepancy, however, lies in the fact that the foreground is occupied by a definite eschatological view, which picks up special prophetic traditions and is then further elaborated by the incorporation of units which are partly related but which are partly heterogeneous. One could say briefly that the underlying eschatological view is based largely on the Book of Ezekiel. For what is described in the opening verses xiv. 1-4 (together with the gloss in xiv. 5) could be simply a summary reproduction of what was stated in the last ten chapters of the Book of Ezekiel, beginning with the attack of the nations in Ezek. xxxviii f. But it is done in such a way that only those features, developed it is true, are emphasized, which have been felt to be essential and sufficient. Whereas in Ezek. xxxviii f., for instance, the nations storming Jerusalem meet their doom on the mountains of Israel, in Zech. xiv. 1-2[44] Jerusalem is conquered, part of the population is destroyed—a clear reference to the preceding passage xiii. 7-9—and then the dramatic climax of Yahweh's epiphany is presented; this is just as important as the destruction of the enemies, although the conflict is not developed in detail. The epiphany of Yahweh is based on Ezek. xliii. 1f., but adds an elucidatory comment insofar as the appearance of Yahweh from the East in Ezekiel is here supplemented by reference to the Mount of Olives. This addition, however, has attracted further additions, in that the cleavage of the Mount of Olives is described more closely. Hence we should perhaps take into account the possibility of additions in xiv. 4b onwards, although xiv. 5b (Yahweh's entrance with his saints) should be allocated to the original stratum.[45] As in Ezek. xliii. 1-7 the description of Yahweh's entrance upon his kingship in Zech. xiv. 9 could have formed the climax; it might be asked, therefore, whether the intervening vv. 6-8 should be treated as original embellishments or later additions, which may be based partly on Ezek. xlvii (the Temple spring), partly on Isa. lx. 19f. (the abolition of night and day and the seasons generally) and on

[44] In xiv. 2 the first person singular is unusual because in the rest of the chapter there is no sign of a divine utterance. Hence Marti suspects a gloss, although this is contested by Sellin, because 'a criterion of this nature is most unreliable in writings of the later period' (p. 580f.). It remains, however, to consider whether the beginning of ch. xii, which was a speech of Yahweh in its original form, could have exercised an influence later. After the announcement of Yahweh in xiii. 7-9 its realization with Yahweh in the third person is much more readily intelligible. From the point of view of sense, therefore, Horst's suggestion (p. 258) that we should read $w^{e^,}\bar{a}sap$ $yhwh$ instead of $w^e\bar{a}sapti$ is probably correct. The juxtaposition of divine and prophetic utterance, which was noticeable in ch. ix–xi, is retained to some extent in ch. xii–xiv also.

[45] Cf. a similar analysis of vv. 1–5 in Elliger, ATD 25, p. 167.

other prophetic passages. It is not critical, therefore, for our present study whether we agree with Sellin, who considers that the original unit in xiv. 1–5, 12, 15–18 has been supplemented either by the author himself or a later hand in xiv. 6–11, 13, 14, 20, 21, or with Elliger, who limits the original parts to xiv. 1–4a (although v. 4a is not free from glosses), 5b, 6–9, 11 (apart from the two initial words), 13, 14 (in part), 16, 17, 19, or with Horst, who takes into account the possibility of 'successive joinings' of separate passages, from which he excludes v. 9 (which emphasizes the kingship of Yahweh), thus bringing vv. 1–5 and 6–11 nearer together. Elliger and Horst have rightly recognized that the section xiv. 16–19 (with or without v. 18) only makes sense from the standpoint of v. 9. The pilgrimage of the survivors to the Feast of Booths at Jerusalem is a change in keeping with the tenor of the whole chapter away from the eschatological idea of a pilgrimage of the nations to Zion (Isa. ii. 2–4; Mic. iv. 1–5). Since the idea of the remnant is here transferred to the Gentile world it must have seemed necessary at a later date to give a fuller account of Yahweh's destructive activity against the Gentiles, a subject that was probably deliberately avoided in the original composition. xiv. 10 (and perhaps xiv. 11 also) should be added to these additions in xiv. 12–15, as well as the concluding verses xiv. 20f., in order to emphasize the exalted position of Jerusalem, thus recalling Isa. ii. If one decides to regard xiv. 9 as the climax of the entire account originally, then xiv. 16–19 (probably without the pedantic special treatment of Egypt in xiv. 18) could be the conclusion (similarly also Elliger). The celebration of the 'ecumenical' Feast of Booths may then be considered as a modification of the great banquet of the nations with which the Isaiah-Apocalypse also closes its eschatological description (Isa. xxv. 6–8). Thus, in this abbreviated compass, which is limited to seven or eight verses at the most, ch. xiv is no longer the detailed description that it appears to be in its present form. It is an undoubtedly independent account based primarily on Ezekiel but also on other prophetic writings; it has been thought out as a conclusion to ch. xiif. and is not substantially different from the other independent units of these chapters in respect of its size. Without going into a detailed discussion of the additions, especially those at the beginning of ch. xii and in ch. xiv, there follows in the first place a brief concluding survey, dealing with the present arrangement of the separate units combined in ch. xii–xiv.

Whereas ch. ix. 1–xi. 3—we shall omit the shepherd allegory in

xi. 4–17 in the interests of clarity and not link it with the sword saying about the shepherd in xiii. 7–9—are heavily dependent on contemporary events and represent the type of earlier eschatology, understanding by 'eschatological' a definitive shaping of the people of God's situation in the sense of a restoration, in which reminiscences of Israel under David probably played a part, in ch. xii–xiv the eschatological aspect is more developed. This can be illustrated briefly from one single feature: Jerusalem, which has no special significance in ch. ix–xi, is now central; it retains the character of a historical entity, but insofar as it is drawn into the fire of judgement and has to experience the severity of God's dealings in the form of enemy conquest, while retaining its significance as the throne of the eschatological kingship of Yahweh, and insofar as it follows the same path as Israel, until, as the tested remnant, it becomes the people of God in the eschatological sense, this Jerusalem finds itself on the way to becoming a new and different sort of Jerusalem. It does not renounce its continuity with the historical Jerusalem, but, as the throne of the king who is coming down from heaven, receives through this epiphany of the world-ruler a corresponding quality. There is no doubt that this was the path which led to the later apocalyptic, but—this is how I attempt to explain to myself the situation of this transitional period—it is not yet the mysterious and allusive style of the apocalyptic literature that confronts us here. The impression of mystery and obscurity is caused by the fact that a series of related but very disparate passages have been combined with the intention of being understood as an artistic whole; but their connecting links cannot be demonstrated from the text of the actual separate sections and have to be inferred; recourse to older elements of tradition and motifs has contributed further to the obscurity. In ch. xii–xiv it seems to have been the idea of salvation in the Book of Ezekiel which was of special importance. Formally there is a certain similarity to ch. ix–xi, insofar as we are confronted once more with the alternation of speeches by Yahweh and the prophets; in ch. xiif. divine speech predominates, even if it has not always been sustained when the independent units have been combined, while in ch. xiv the account draws chiefly on prophetic speech.

Thus, the eschatological composition begins with a brief introduction, sketching the external position of Jerusalem in the light of the attack of the nations (xii. 2a, 4a, 3a) before turning immediately to the internal situation at Jerusalem (xii. 9f.), while externally the crisis begins at the same moment that Yahweh strives to destroy the army of the nations. The influence of these events does, in fact, lead to a change of heart on the part of the inhabitants of Jerusalem, which is why the prophetic picture of the outpuring of the divine spirit can easily be used; but—interpreting xii. 10 in conjunction with xii. 11 in this way—the inhabitants of Jerusalem looked at transgressions which had taken place in the past and had required a corresponding act of atonement, and they therefore arranged a great day of repentance according to the customary rites (xii. 11–14). The aim of this lament was purification from sin and uncleanness; the atonement ritual had at its disposal a reliable source for removing the vessels of unclean spirit, idol-worship and degenerate prophecy; use had, in fact, been made of it from time to time but was now attended with definite success (xiii. 1–6). The author of Zech. xii–xiv is quite convinced of the justification for acting in this way, but in view of the eschatological situation he seems to consider this procedure, hitherto regarded as self-evident, completely inadequate; it does not take into account the severity and intensity of Yahweh's eschatological activity. Yahweh's announcement in xiii. 7–9 is all the more fearsome, therefore; it spares neither the shepherd nor the little ones and subjects even the remaining third to purification by fire. The absence of any further announcement by Yahweh, about the position of the surviving remnant for instance, is very effective. In its place the fulfilment of what has been announced is described briefly in an independent section (xiv. 1–2), until destructive, hostile activity against Jerusalem is curtailed without a blow by the epiphany of Yahweh from the Mount of Olives (xiv. 3, 4a, 5b); the epiphany reaches its climax in Yahweh's entrance upon his kingship (xiv. 9). Because the idea of the remnant is transferred to the Gentile world in a most unusual manner, the account is able to arrive at a comforting conclusion in the form of a universal Feast of Booths (xiv. 16–19, probably without xiv. 18).

The distinctive mark of this eschatological composition, in my opinion, lies in the retention of the dogma of the post-exilic community regarding the exceptional position of Israel because it was founded on cult and law, a dogma found for instance in the Chronicler's work of history where it appears as the ultimate goal, and its renewed combination with the idea of the remnant, which is still considered valid though not yet finally realized. This, then, is another case of the divorce between the view which regards the expectation of the earlier prophets as already realized in the existence of the present community and is consequently indifferent or antagonistic to a contemporary eschatology, and the eschatological faith which is always waiting for the realization of the prophetic promises and which can only reply to the view represented by the official church by sharpening and intensifying the eschatological situation through a revived use of the idea of the remnant. But this answer is given in the ritual language with which the official community is also familiar; it is not without reason, therefore, that it is based on the Book of Ezekiel and the eschatological features in the model constitution drawn up by Ezekiel (xliii. 1f.) are picked up and stressed. Likewise, in view of the importance which Jerusalem and the Temple hold in the preaching of Haggai and Zechariah—both prophets are also grouped together in the work of the Chronicler—the addition of this composition (ch. xii–xiv) to the Book of Zechariah is easy to understand.

In comparison with the Isaiah-Apocalypse the views put forward in Zech. xii–xiv give the impression of belonging to an earlier period. The eschatological groups are already entrenched to a certain extent; but whereas the Isaiah-Apocalypse—insofar as a terminal stage is discernible in ch. xxiv–xxvi—reveals hostility to the opponents of the eschatological faith, and at the same time internal debate over problems within their own ranks, such as incipient doubts and temptations, here in Zech. xii–xiv the relationship to the official church seems to be somewhat closer; contrary views are encountered without any surrender of personal convictions, but there is an attempt to strengthen these convictions by increasing the eschatological emphasis. If we might be permitted to give a closer definition of the situation in which our passage could have been composed by linking it with a contemporary event, we could cite the Samaritan schism, if the usual dating of this extremely significant event between 350 and 300 B.C. is correct. Some decades later, but certainly not before the publication of the Chronicler's work, Zech. xii–xiv could have contained the reply of the eschatological groups to the Chronicler's theology of history and could have contributed considerably to the sharpening of already existing differences. If, then, Zech. xii–xiv can be brought down into the first decades of the third century, we should think in terms of the closing decades of the same century for the period when the Isaiah-Apocalypse was composed.

We must add a few words about the numerous glosses in Zech. xii and xiv. The secondary clauses which have been added to ch. xiv are not so important. Without exception they clarify or complete the sense, and sometimes evidence a much narrower and more anxious attitude. xiv. 4b, 5, 6a (concluding with a historical reminiscence of the earthquake under King Uzziah) would belong to this category; the miraculous cleavage of the Mount of Olives required a comment which would also agree with the changed position of the Hinnom valley without mentioning it by name. In recollection of the exalted position of Mount Zion in the expectations of Isa. ii. 2–4, a similar emphasis is transferred to the whole of Jerusalem—in contrast to the countryside of Judah—by means of a brief sketch of the city's environs (xiv. 10f.). Verses 12–15, which are not without internal contradictions (cf. xiv. 12 and xiv. 13), regard an additional description of the enemy's destruction as necessary and hence do not form a very good transition to the universal Feast of Booths in xiv. 16f. This passage (xiv. 16–19) has also been expanded by pedantic consideration for Egypt in xiv. 18. The final verses of the chapter (xiv. 20f.) emphasize the cultic purity of the new Jerusalem in two particular respects, thus underlining what may have been taken for granted by the eschatological groups. In spite of the mounting degree of holiness there is no denying the impression of a slight uncertainty. Whether vv. 6–8 belonged to the original strand may be left open; xiv. 9, at any rate, would be more effective if joined to xiv. 5b.

Less easy to explain, however, are the additions to xii. 1–8 (in its present form), which must have grown round the isolated verse xiv. 4a. xii. 2b, 3b, 4bα (with a gloss in 4bβ), 5–8 belong to this addition. The theme throughout is the obscure relationship of the country areas of Judah to Jerusalem, which is afflicted by the eschatological attack of the nations. It is not clear whether Judah is at first on the side of Jerusalem's enemies, before it undergoes a change of heart and becomes the scene of the enemies' destruction, so that afterwards there is no reason for Jerusalem to be haughty towards Judah, or whether these additional clauses are meant to answer the very natural question, how the countryside (Judah) will fare in this eschatological event which is so exclusively concerned with Jerusalem. In the middle of the shepherd allegory preceding ch. xii, which we omitted previously on the grounds that it was probably an eschatological interpretation of contemporary events no longer open to investigation and was preparing the way for the transition to ch. xii–xiv, there is an event which reminds us of the symbolic acts of the prophets. Two staves, which illustrate the covenant of Yahweh with the nations and the fraternal covenant between Judah and Ephraim, are broken. Some manuscripts of the Septuagint[46]—

[46] These are the manuscripts G 62. 147 in the enumeration of Holmes-Parsons.

certainly incorrectly—read 'Jerusalem' for 'Israel' in two cases and thus make it clear that carrying over the message of xi. 4–17 to xii. 1–8, they would regard the relationship of Judah to Jerusalem in xii. 1–8 as hostile. Apart from this a similar situation could be inferred from xiv. 10. We have denoted this verse as a later addition; but it could be that the reduction of Jewish territory (in its pre-Josianic compass) to the plain of the Arabah, i.e. the Jordan valley, could be understood as a punishment for initial wavering on the part of Judah. It seems to me, therefore, that the additions in xii. 1–8 reflect the changes of a tense relationship between Judah and Jerusalem, possibly going back to certain experiences during the third century B.C. which are no longer accessible in detail. There was probably some connection with the special significance that was gradually attributed to Jerusalem in the expected eschatological event. In order to understand what ch. xii–xiv wish to say when the glosses have been removed, these additions do not need to be considered to begin with. They serve to indicate, however, that certain events—even if they were peripheral—were noted and recorded by these eschatological groups and were made to fit their expectations of the future more or less suitably.

3. JOEL

For the questions we are discussing in the present study it is particularly the two final chapters of the Book of Joel (according to the enumeration of the Hebrew text) that are of interest. But since the connection of these two chapters with ch. i and ii is regarded differently, a reference to the situation of the whole book cannot be avoided altogether. This can be done briefly by basing it on the general outline which has become accepted—with slight variations—in the course of the last few decades in the interpreation of the Book of Joel.[47]

There is no doubt that ch. iii and iv are to be interpreted as prophecy. The only way, therefore, to maintain the unity of the whole book seemed to be the way suggested particularly by Merx[48] and other scholars of the earlier period, namely to understand the first two chapters also in a similar sense. In view of the untenability

[47] Cf. the very instructive survey in Eissfeldt, pp. 391ff.
[48] A. Merx, *Die Prophetie des Joel und ihre Ausleger von den ältesten Zeiten bis zu den Reformatoren* (1879).

of this position most commentators following Wellhausen have thought it more appropriate to divide the book.[49] But this seemed to necessitate agreement with the view put forward by Duhm and others, namely that statements in ch. i and ii referring to the future day of Yahweh should be regarded as later insertions, reinterpretations in the sense of ch. iiif., or alternatively, in the light of the stylistic and thematic connection of these additions with the neighbouring verses, it seemed to require at least a modified version of this view, namely that the references to the day of Yahweh which are to be found in ch. if. are, in fact, seeking to illustrate only the extent of the contemporary need and that the contemporary plague of locusts is a picture of the distress on the day of Yahweh. This pointed the way to a clearer view of the unity of the Book of Joel.[50] According to Weiser, for instance, Joel recorded the message which he delivered at that time and which is contained in ch. i and ii after the end of the plague of locusts and the drought, before adding ch. iii and iv as a supplement to the references to the day of Yahweh mentioned in ch. i and ii. Kapelrud[51] wishes to interpret the book as the liturgy of a cult-prophet and refers to Ugaritic texts in interpreting it against the background of Canaanite fertility cults and the eschatological festival of Yahweh's accession to the throne. Even so, however, arguments for the unity of the book have to acknowledge that on a limited scale, at least, we must reckon with eschatological-apocalyptic and other additions, especially in ch. iiif.[52]

From this rough survey it may be inferred that at present a sharp distinction between the eschatological sections in ch. iii and iv and the chapters dealing with a plague of locusts and drought is not recommended, nor is the transition from ch. if. to ch. iii and iv, which were once arranged differently, smoothed away in order to preserve the unity of the book at all costs; hence, there stands before us as author a man in whose heart very different expressions of Old Testament piety lay side by side. For posterity, at any rate, the eschatological side of this piety carried greater weight and it was only because of these sections which are contained in the last

---

[49] So K. Marti, *Das Dodekapropheton*, KHC XIII (1904); W. Nowack, *Die kleinen Propheten*, HK III no. 4 (1922³); E. Sellin, *Das Zwölfprophetenbuch*, KAT XII no. 1 (1929–30², ³); T. H. Robinson, *Die zwölf kleinen Propheten*, HAT I no. 14 (1954²).
[50] Cf. the attempt of A. Weiser, *Das Buch der zwölf kleinen Propheten*, ATD 24 no. 1 (1952²).
[51] A. S. Kapelrud, *Joel Studies* (1948).
[52] Thus, for instance, A. Jepsen, 'Kleine Beiträge zum Zwölfprophetenbuch', *ZAW* 56 (1938), pp. 85–96.

two chapters that the book was preserved as a prophetic writing and later received into the prophetic canon.

To understand these eschatological sections, however, it is necessary to preface our remarks with a brief consideration of the first two chapters, without a lengthy discussion at this point of the resulting literary-critical questions. We begin by picking up Weiser's point (ATD, p. 89) that the basis of ch. i and ii is concerned with the later record of what 'Joel' had said as a result of an almost unique plague of locusts. It is true that we are no longer in a position to draw a clear dividing line between what he said originally and the later written record, but we must bear in mind the possibility that when it came to be written down later the oral message was expanded by embellishments and exaggerations of the distress now happily overcome. One of the primary elements of this later arrangement of the oral message, which could hardly have contained more than now stands in i. 4–10, for instance, with a challenge to fast similar to the message in the written form of i. 1–14 or ii. 12–14, 12–18, was the embellished interpretation of these terrible events by means of prophetic, theological reflection about the day of Yahweh in ii. 1b and 2 and ii. 11; the day of Yahweh, however, was linked with an extended and almost platitudinous description of the plague of locusts, so that the locusts are now introduced as if they were the eschatological enemies that belong to the source-material of the day of Yahweh; thus, in ii. 10, for instance, the swarm of locusts reminds one of an eclipse of sun and moon. The subsequent challenge to fast and repent, which makes free use of essentially similar expressions (ii. 12f.), leads to the divine promise (ii. 19–20), which in ii. 20 reveals clear connections with the plague of locusts.

There are also some verses in ch. i and ii that undoubtedly refer to a plague and should be linked with these later additions, which are probably connected with the written stage of tradition; i. 11–18, together with the concluding prayer in i. 19–20, also belong here. In contrast to the verses which refer to a plague of locusts, they should be thought of as independent,[53] although they really belong

[53] Cf. for instance what Robinson (HAT) says on i. 11 f., whereas Weiser does not recommend any division into words about drought and words about locusts, if the double catastrophe is then taken to imply derivation from two different authors (ATD, p. 101); this is not necessary, in fact, although it should not exclude the possibility that the two dangerous natural catastrophes of Palestine have probably been joined together at this point by the same author in the form of a summary appendix. A similar view is held by Jepsen, who separates the verses about drought, which he thinks begin in i. 8, from the verses about the plague of locusts, although he derives both series from an author whom he would like to place at the time of the exile.

in the vicinity of the plague of locusts, insofar as the consequences
of a drought constitute a similar threat to human existence as the
results of a plague of locusts. This implies a certain similarity
between the two great possible natural catastrophes that are always
recurring in Palestine; in i. 15, in what is probably a fragmentary
section dealing with drought, the day of Yahweh is referred to as an
illustrative element, although it is much more loosely connected
with the neighbouring verses[54] in my opinion than the day of Yahweh
in ch. ii is related to the plague of locusts. At all events the
concluding exhortation to rejoice in ii. 21–27 takes account of both
forms of catastrophe, while praising Yahweh as the one who brings
the distress of drought to an end by sending rain and who alleviates
the ravages of the plague of locusts, so that it is quite possible that
both threats to human existence may have emerged together.[55] In
each case it is followed by Yahweh's restoration which is connected
with the cultic-ritual measures of the Zion community that have
been provided for such catastrophes. Perhaps it is mistaken to recall
the first two visions of the Book of Amos (Amos vii. 1–3, 4–6), in
which the coming judgement on Israel is likewise thought of in the
form of a plague of locusts and widespread drought. But it is probably
not accidental that both threats are averted by prophetic intervention,
without definitely putting an end to the coming judgement; we
know that the prophet cannot intercede further in view of the
prophecies of judgement in the following visions (Amos vii. 7, 8;
viii. 1f.). The first two chapters of the Book of Joel are understandably limited to the catastrophes threatened in the first two visions
of the Book of Amos, but it is indicative that here instead of the
prophetic intervention the cult community itself intervenes with the
help of the usual cultic-ritual measures, in which a 'cult-prophetic
figure' may have played an incidental part, although his significance
was already predetermined by the fixed cultic ritual and was certainly
very modest. For it is not the 'cult-prophet' who intervenes so much
as the whole community, which draws on the help of the cult, in
which a prophetic figure or else a cultic official can act as the spokesman. Thus, natural and recurrent catastrophes, such as Amos also
experienced and which he interpreted in a prophetic-eschatological
manner, are again felt to be natural times of distress which can be
withstood and overcome by firm faith with the help of the cult,

---

[54] Jepsen is probably thinking particularly of this verse when he feels that the
sentences referring to the day of Yahweh are disruptive on the whole.
[55] Sellin had already referred to this in KAT, p. 153.

which was instituted and is maintained for this purpose. The references to the day of Yahweh in ch. i and iii should also be understood from this point of view. They contain a kerugmatic element from the earlier prophets (Amos, Zephaniah), which now serves as a graphic illustration of contemporary distresses and afflictions and seeks to point expressly to the fact that in harmony with the faith of the old prophets, now consummated in the cult, Yahweh's help and his gracious, protecting presence should be entreated. Thus, these statements about the day of Yahweh that were previously understood eschatologically have been adopted by a later period in this non-eschatological form, so that Yahweh's promise of restoration, which was received in the course of the cultic measures, was retained in the final version just as it had been announced in ii. 19f. This promise may stem from the mouth of a man who understood himself as a prophet, although apart from the name he has little in common with the opposition prophets of an earlier period, whose sayings he utilized. He obviously tried to give the modest rôle he played at that time greater significance by means of a later account; hence we have a record of events at that time. Events of a similar nature were certainly not unusual; hence, we may suspect there was a special reason for making the written record of such a very ordinary event into a prophetic writing, which was later deemed worthy to be received into the prophetic canon. This reason must be sought indirectly in the last two chapters of the Book of Joel.

The metaphorical statements about the day of Yahweh in ch. i and ii were now, of course, prophetic revelations, once uttered at the command of Yahweh, and even in their metaphorical-liturgical use they had not completely lost their innate power to represent words of Yahweh. At all events, in circles which still retained their respect for the old prophetic word the message of the earlier prophets, although only serving as illustration, provoked definite reactions, namely to hold fast to the eschatological meaning of certain parts of the prophetic message and to attain to a new historico-eschatological interpretation of this message. The addition of ch. iii and iv to Joel i and ii and hence the formation of the present Book of Joel as a prophetic writing is to be understood from this point of view.

On the other hand, this suggests a certain antithesis in the relation of the two main parts of the Book of Joel, which does not favour the assumption that we are still dealing with the same author in

ch. iii and iv, or at least in certain parts of ch. iv,[56] as in ch. i and ii.
Assuming that ii. 27 formed a conclusion which was not expected
to be continued, it seems worth considering the possibility of a
development in two stages in interpreting ch. iii and iv. The first stage
is to be found in ch. iv. The primary aim of these additions is the
restoration or confirmation of the eschatological interpretation of
the remarks about the day of Yahweh which appear in ch. i and ii.
Since the description of the plague of locusts in ch. ii was based
on the comparison with human troops, because of the references
to the day of Yahweh, the transition to enemy peoples was not
too difficult. iv. 1 is undoubtedly a prose introduction, as Robinson
(HAT, *loc. cit.*) holds, without it necessarily being secondary; the
verse should be understood as a bridge from ii. 27 and points to
the fact that the final restoration of Israel should be discussed in
the form of a concluding historical act of Yahweh. The connected
sections iv. 1-3 and iv. 9f. are related to each other as a theme
occasioned by regard for historical events is related to its development. As a result of the link with ch. ii the development itself is
marked by a military emphasis, which is clearly a deliberate reversal
of the peaceful description in Isa. ii. 4 (Mic. iv. 3); it is a stirring
reminder that the restoration of Israel cannot be attained by a
painless continuation of the present situation, but only by a martial
encounter, for which Israel must be prepared. There is a deliberate
reference in iv. 15 to ii. 10; but what is understood in iv. 15 as an
illustrative picture is interpreted in ii. 10 as an eschatological event,
without which the final restoration is inconceivable. It might be
objected that the description of the End in iv. 17, together with the
account of salvation in iv. 18, both derived from the eschatological
interpretation, is not so very different from what is promised in ii. 19
and is held out to the people in ii. 23f. in the summons to rejoice.
But there is a difference between such a situation being promised as a
consequence of cultic piety, despite the permanent contradiction with
actual reality, and being interpreted eschatologically as the ultimate
conclusion of Yahweh's activity in history. This is precisely what the
additions in ch. iv wish to emphasize; they are not yet in fundamental
opposition to the result which is the ideal of ch. i and ii; but they insist
upon a necessary addition. Cultic piety is not attacked or ignored,
but it is the eschatological expectation that gives it its significance.

[56] Thus, for instance, C. Kuhl, *The Old Testament: Its Origins and Composition*
(1961), pp. 204 ff.; he thinks that the author of the prophetic liturgy in ch. i and ii
is still at work in iv. 1-3 and iv. 9-20, but he regards the prose passage iv. 4-8
(together with the final promise in iv. 21) and also ch. iii as secondary embellishments.

The prose section iv. 4–8 seems to have been added for the sake of concrete explanation. Whereas in iv. 1–3 the nations are spoken of in a general sense, in iv. 4–8 specific events connected with Sidon, Tyre etc. are thought of. It will be wise, therefore, not to regard the mention of the Ionians in iv. 6 as an indication of date for all eschatological sections, but only for the insertion iv. 4–8, which probably derives from the Hellenistic period. Likewise in iv. 19 and 21, or in iv. 21 alone, we may be dealing with secondary embellishments.

Thus, the most important sections of ch. iv represent the first act of a renewed attempt to give an eschatological character to ideas about the day of Yahweh and events connected with it; undoubtedly these were once understood eschatologically, but within the cultically based community of the post-exilic period they served simply to illustrate present afflictions, which could be withstood and overcome by the approved path of cultic observances. A further step is visible in the insertion of ch. iii.

The question posed by the general indication of time in iii. 1, namely how ch. iii came into its present position between ch. ii and iv, will be omitted to begin with. Chapter iii itself is to be thought of as a unity; it is true that it combines different ideas, a not unusual trait among eschatological sections; but there are no grounds for assuming two apocalyptic fragments (iii. 1–2; iii, 3–5), as Robinson does. Similarly, Jepsen's division into divine and prophetic utterance, with its conclusion that apocalyptic additions may be discerned in the parts which form the prophetic utterance (iii. 4f.), is not very convincing. There is nothing against including iii. 4 also in the divine utterance; for the expression 'day of Yahweh' is so formal that it is quite in keeping with a speech of Yahweh. iii. 5 probably contains an explanation, as may be perceived in the introductory phrase *weḥāyāh*; nevertheless, the verse should not be regarded as a later addition but as a concluding explanation and summary of the various ideas already referred to. The central point of iii. 1f. is the outpouring of the divine spirit. This was not something new in Israel, but in the past it had been limited to individuals who were witnesses to the presence of Yahweh by their possession of the spirit, although it had been understood by the prophets, especially Ezekiel, and also in passages like Num. xi. 16f (cf. xi. 29), as an eschatological event, an expression of the close union between Israel and its God. iii. 1f. seeks to express the whole idea of the outpouring of the spirit in such a way that the otherwise important differences in age, together with the differences between the sexes, lose their relevance, just as the very various modes of revelation, each valued differently in the past, are equated in a general way. Robinson rightly points to passages like Dan. v. 11 and 14, 'where the ability to interpret dreams is attributed to the power of God' (HAT, p. 66).[57] But the sign of the outpouring of the spirit which characterizes eschatological Israel is also implicitly connected with separation and cleavage. There is no doubt that *kol baśar* refers to the whole house of Israel; it is equally obvious that only the Israel that is directed and guided by such eschatological expectation can be addressed as the eschatological Israel. The deliberate emphasis on the outpuring of the spirit as important for the Israel of the last days suggests that such an expectation was by no means generally shared in Israel. The point of iii. 3–4 lies in the contrast it provides to the statement in iii. 1. These verses paint a dark picture of the day of Yahweh and its disastrous consequences for the world, unless it has been set apart by the outpouring of the spirit. At the same time these statements are to be understood as chronological pointers: what is foretold in iii. 1 will become reality on the terrible day of Yahweh. The simultaneity of the events within (iii. 1) and without (iii. 3f.) Israel obviously required special explanation, however; this is now given in iii. 5. It not only locates the outpouring of the spirit on Zion, but it also describes the saving activity of the outpouring of the spirit in the invocation of Yahweh. It is true that the technical term which had grown up in the cult was used for this purpose, but the point contained in it seems unmistakable to me: only the invocation of Yahweh that is based on the activity of the spirit, i.e., only the confession of faith pronounced by the eschatological Israel, guarantees deliverance, as iii. 5bβ expressly underlines: 'and only those whom Yahweh calls (viz., by the outpouring of the spirit) will escape'.[58] This seems to me the special importance of iii. 5, namely that a hidden division of Israel is being prepared. Deliverance on the day of Yahweh is still promised to all Israel, but this must mean the Israel that has responded to the eschatological faith and considers the day of Yahweh as an eschatological entity.

We must now examine the factors that contributed to the present position of ch. iii. In comparison with ch. i and ch. iv, ch. iii seems to be *sui generis*. But this is not easy to demonstrate from the point of view of content. In content the various statements of the chapter

[57] iii. 2 must be a later addition which multiplies the differences already referred to; even social differences cannot limit the outpouring of the spirit.

[58] Cf. the emendation recently proposed again by Robinson (HAT, *loc. cit.*), reading *weśaredû* instead of *ûbaśśeridîm*.

agree to a large extent with statements from other eschatological sections in the prophetic books; in fact, at a first glance ch. iii might be regarded as a variant to iv. 15f.; but the emphasis is quite different. The additional new factor, the outpouring of the spirit, does, it is true, stem from prophetic traditions, but it has special importance, in fact, exclusive importance, in its context. All Israel is still addressed as the eschatological people; but in the outpouring of the spirit a visible sign of this eschatological Israel is named; the fact that it is thought necessary to mention such a sign points to a conventicle-type limitation even in the initial stages. If the eschatological Israel is a visible unit marked by specific features, then this affects the present also, insofar as only those who give expression to their acceptance of the eschatological faith will participate in the deliverance of the eschatological Israel. Here, then, lie the beginnings of the path which leads to the later apocalyptic.

At first the only aim behind the collecting, supplementing and re-arranging of eschatological traditions was to keep alive something which had been proclaimed as the prophetic word of Yahweh and to use this to strengthen their own faith. Resistance to the contemporary significance of the eschatological interpretation of events, especially since the establishment of the Jewish community, which to a considerable degree based its unique position and significance in the world on its claim to be the Israel of the old prophetic promise rescued by the last Judgement, led to the limitation of eschatological expectation to the circle of those who were convinced of the contemporary validity of the eschatological faith and wished to establish it in their midst. Chapter iii, it seems to me, seeks to do this. It is always hazardous to try to date eschatological passages even approximately if there is no incontestable evidence; in Joel iii and iv this is only true of iv. 4–8, which is generally and rightly regarded as a gloss from the Greek period. This much, however, can be said: the combination of the most important passages in ch. iv (1–3, 9–14, 15–17, 18–20), a process inconceivable without embellishment, preceded the insertion of ch. iii. The exclusive character of the eschatological Israel, marked by the outpouring of the spirit, seems to presuppose the establishment of the post-exilic community, namely the period of Ezra and Nehemiah. The indeterminate chronological reference in iii. 1, loosely connected with ii. 27, seeks to give warning emphasis that the hopes of restoration, originally an innocent addition, as brought together in ch. iv, only make sense if they relate to the Israel which was committed to the eschatological faith. There can hardly be any great chronological difference between ch. if. and ch. iv. But we shall probably never succeed in giving a compelling date for the Book of Joel in its earlier form, consisting of ch. i, ii and iv. Apart from the later embellishments of his apocalyptist, Jepsen has suggested the first decades of the Exile.[59] The interiorization of repentance by the use of prophetic expressions (cf. ii. 13) could, in view of the Book of Malachi's criticisms of the priesthood for forgetting their duties, point to the decades after the restoration of the Temple prior to the emergence of Ezra and Nehemiah; in fact, there is no compelling reason against coming down to the initial period after the establishment of the Jewish community. The insertion of ch. iii, however, should probably be thought of independently of the events which are connected with the names of Ezra and Nehemiah, so that the earliest date that could be suggested for the Book of Joel in its present form—apart from slight additions in ch. iv—is the last century of Persian rule. This seems to have been the century in which increasing weight was attached to the question whether, following the formation of the Jewish community, there was still a place for eschatological expectation in a theocratic community that was based on certain definite assumptions. The conflicting views, however, do not seem to be so fixed as one might infer from Zech. xii–xiv or the Isaiah-Apocalypse as a result of the Chronicler's view of history. Hence, Joel iii and indeed the whole book in its present form—apart from iv. 4–8 and some glosses at the end of ch. iv—may be linked with the period from the foundation of the Jewish community prior to the publication of the Chronicler's history (i.e., the period between 400 and 330).

Thus, our discussion of three selected independent units of eschatological content seeks to draw a distinction within prophecy, a distinction which can be traced backwards from the Book of Daniel via the 'Isaiah-Apocalypse' and 'Trito-Zechariah' to Joel iii. We are probably justified in rounding off with a brief sketch of this line of development, although it runs counter to the stream of history in the sense of historical sequence, and in appending some conclusions which in my opinion go further and whose development must be the subject of a further examination. This will require us to make some additions as well as modifications to our account in Chapter 3 which was put forward as an unproven hypothesis and was preparatory to the interpretation of the texts discussed in the present chapter.

[59] Cf. *ZAW* 56, pp. 90f.

H

CHAPTER V

THEOCRACY AND ESCHATOLOGY

THE analysis of these three larger eschatological units comprises only a small selection from a large number of similar promises in other prophetic writings. Zech. ix–xi was touched on in our discussion of Zech. xii–xiv. The complicated structure of the Book of Micah—nothing but threats in the first three chapters, followed by promises in ch. iv and at the beginning of ch. v, succeeded by further threats in the remainder of the chapter and in ch. vi, while the main part of ch. vii has the character of promise once more—would certainly have tempted us to include this prophetic writing in our examination. This would also apply to other eschatological units which—like Isa. xxxiii or Isa. xxxiv–v, for instance—are comparatively compact. But, although it was originally our intention to do this, it did not seem wise to try to examine every single piece of eschatological material in the writings of the prophets. Therefore, we took the step of choosing a limited number of such units, which, in comparison with neighbouring eschatological sections, give fairly uniform evidence of a more developed structure or sharper definition of the eschatological aspect, or which are to be considered as independent units that have no reference to preceding or subsequent verses.

The eschatological part of the Book of Joel may be understood as a supplementary section. The expression 'day of Yahweh' in ch. i and ii, which is derived from the eschatological picture-book and has been selected in order to illustrate contemporary needs, is confirmed in its historico-eschatological interpretation by the future expectations of Joel ch. iv. The martial features which are peculiar to iv. 9f. serve as a warning that earlier statements about Israel's future should only continue to be used as illustrative metaphors, because in their original form they tell of a future reality which cannot be attained, in fact, without confusion and conflict. The later insertion of ch. iii is a clear indication of restriction; there is no doubt that the hopes expressed in ch. iv will come true, but these expectations only apply to Israel, which draws its life from the eschatological faith and which is characterized as eschatological by the outpouring of the spirit. This could, of course, be the empirical Israel of the period from which Joel iii stems; but the possibility that the two entities, empirical and eschatological Israel, are no longer self-evidently identical seems to be envisaged. Obviously there was no lack of protest in the meantime regarding a realization of eschatological expectations; hence, a restriction of the sort evident in Joel iii was considered necessary.

A similar development may be assumed in the case of the additions to the Book of Zechariah. The hopes that find expression in Zech. ix. 1–xi. 3 signify in the first place a resumption and development of what was presented as directly imminent in the visions of Proto-Zechariah. They make it clear that the pattern of these hopes was the result of certain political events, probably in the last two decades of Persian rule, and they emphasize again that the fulfilment of these hopes cannot be expected without military complications. The shepherd allegory in ch. xi. 4f., which was passed over because not all the details are clear to us, has in view not only the dissolution of the covenant between Judah and Ephraim but also the events connected with the emergence of Alexander and the overthrow of Persian rule and the not unrelated Samaritan schism. The shepherd narrative presumably aims at entering into the military complications which were reported in ch. ix. 1–xi. 3. The kernel of ch. xii–xiv, which is overloaded with various additions, seeks to confirm this understanding of historical events by intensifying the eschatological aspect. Whereas the cultic community is of the opinion that it can remain untouched by historical afflictions if it resorts to the approved cultic-ritual measures, the eschatological group proclaims that judgement is being meted out against Jerusalem and addresses the remnant that survives this judgement as the eschatological Israel, which will experience the entry of the heavenly king into Jerusalem, his consecrated city.

The Isaiah-Apocalypse is even more unequivocal and clear. It is reasonable to assume that its beginnings were connected with expectation of the eschatological revolution—again on the ground of historical tribulation, but in this case tribulation long past, which had been judged to be preliminary and not final. In contrast, the eschatological catastrophe is now regarded as a cosmic event and the disarmament of rebellious heavenly powers is linked with the overthrow of earthly rulers who are hostile to Yahweh. Israel only appears rehabilitated on Zion when the banquet of the nations is celebrated. At the same time, however, obviously to dispel doubt within the eschatological groups, the eschatological faith is described

H§

as the way of the righteous and the conquest of death is presented as the event which will mark the eschatological revolution in its finality. Appended to these admonitions and assurances, the content of which, in comparison with the preceding verses, is very similar to the Book of Daniel, are older hopes of restoration in ch. xxvii in the form of postscripts, undoubtedly a retrograde step when compared with the position already attained, but understandable in view of the effort not to leave unmentioned any of the traditions which were felt to be important. The consequent disharmony was taken as part of the price for duly preserving room for quite traditional, entrenched expectations, such as the re-unification of Israel and the return of the Diaspora.

A selection has been made, therefore, of eschatological passages that might serve as guiding points to produce a line, when joined together, that leads from the older restoration eschatology, which is certainly within the sphere of influence of the pre-exilic prophetic promises, to the rather different, dualistic and apocalyptic form of eschatology, such as we find in a fairly complete form in the Book of Daniel. This line is not without gaps; intervening parts must be hypothetically and experimentally filled in; nor is it straight and consistent; sometimes it takes several steps backwards or halts at a point reached previously. Above all we must reject the false assumption that we are thinking about a line characterized by a forward-pressing development, a line which had consciously left the previous stages of development behind. Elements of the older restoration eschatology that envisage a definitive pattern of historical relationships, i.e. a consummation of this earthly world with Israel in the centre, are constantly re-appearing. But these elements were increasingly re-interpreted by more modern ideas, on which naturally greater emphasis was placed, until the dualistic world picture stands before us, a picture characterized by the end of the present aeon and the coming of the new aeon, which seems to be reserved solely for Israel, or what was gradually understood by 'Israel'. It is these changes in Israel's understanding of itself in the long course of its history that are perhaps responsible for the fact that the eschatological expectations cannot be brought under a single denominator. Although the influences emanating from foreign sources or from historical-political changes are undeniable, the actual occasion within the Old Testament that must be adduced to explain the eschatological change of structure probably lies here in the changing understanding of what Israel is— a cultic community, a nation, a theocracy. If we might risk a 'terrible simplification' to describe the period under discussion, we might well say that the tension between theocracy and eschatology must have played a special rôle. Can a theocracy, which regards itself not as a specially exalted nation alongside other nations but as a divine creation, incommensurable in terms of this world, a theocracy, in fact, which interprets its existence as the fulfilment of definite promises which Yahweh had once announced by the mouth of the prophets, take seriously an historical eschatology, according to which substantially more would be given to it than it already possessed? It can, of course, make use of older eschatological ideas to illustrate its present situation; but it can hardly endow them with historical influence, at any rate not in comparison with the principles, delivered to it at its foundation, which determine its present existence. Yet this seems to have been the way Israel was understood in the circles represented by men like Ezra and Nehemiah when they executed their mission in Jerusalem. It was primarily a work of consolidating the situation created by the dissolution of national sovereignty and not yet settled even in the first decades of Persian rule. A substantial contribution to the unrest was probably made by the restoration eschatology, which in the dark years of the exile had been the hope and mainstay of the 'Pious' and which had certainly not been silenced by the rebuilding of the Temple, as some of the Diaspora may have hoped; in fact, it had perhaps even gained in strength. Ultimately, however, this continuation of the restoration eschatology signified the consolidation of a condition of suspense and uncertainty, which was unfavourable to any attempt to regulate the situation with definiteness and led instead to a provisional acceptance of whatever happened to be the position, the final solution being left to a future initiative on Yahweh's part. The only way to neutralize such influences was not by combating or discrediting living eschatological hopes, which might perhaps only have provoked fresh tensions, but by burying them in the foundations of the community which was to be rebuilt, the unique and incomparable significance of which could be understood *inter alia* as the fulfilment of prophetic promises. In plain language, the Priestly Writing's interpretation of history, *viz.* that Yahweh's activity among men had found its culmination in the founding of the theocracy of Israel on Sinai, could avail itself of the prophetic-eschatological message, insofar as the long interval between the founding of the theocracy on Sinai and its re-establishment under Ezra and Nehemiah could be bridged with the help of the prophetic message. Here lie the roots of the later view, represented especially by the Pharisees, that the prophets were to be understood as transmitters and interpreters of the law; a definite interest, therefore, by the leading circles of the Jewish theocracy in collecting the productions of the prophetic spirit is easy to understand. In this way, however, the importance of prophecy, especially of the eschatological side of its message, was restricted to a particular period of the past. Thus the tombs of the prophets could be adorned with pious worship, by expressly emphasizing their importance in the past, without having to grant contemporary importance to the eschatological message of the earlier prophets. This marks out a path which a theocracy can tread without being endangered by the disturbing force of eschatological hopes.

But the collection of prophetic traditions, already partly begun by the prophets themselves 'for testimony and instruction' (Isa. viii. 16, 20), could also have been pursued on other assumptions. There were, of course, words of Yahweh which had once been proclaimed by the prophets of old, divine promises which could not remain unfulfilled, but whose fulfilment—in view of what they proclaimed and in view of what had actually been attained—must still have been anticipated as imminent. From this point of view the prophetic word, especially as a word of promise, still commanded respect. A collection of prophetic traditions undertaken on these assumptions must have given quite a different impression, therefore. Such a collection would be made not to seal off a past epoch of religious history, or at the most to see in the prophetic witnesses models and instructors in the faith, but to interpret the testimonies already collected so that men could live by them, ready for the future that was dawning. The circles which we connect with this type of collection of prophetic writing cannot simply be identified with the leading circles of the theocracy, although there certainly must have been connections from both sides. We have no proper name for these collectors and interpreters of prophetic traditions and can only surmise where they actually came from. Only a hypothetical picture, therefore, can be given of them, although, in my opinion, such a picture does justice to the historical situation with some probability. We take them, then, to be the eschatological groups and, without attributing special weight to the question at this juncture, we place their origins in those decades of the exilic and early post-exilic period when, under the impact of the prophets' message of judgement, hope of ancient Israel's recovery and restoration was probably still entertained by large groups of society. It would not be mistaken to link them with the deuteronomic-deuteronomistic movement, but we should then have to regard them as the eschatological wing of the agitation for renewal, as expressed for a time in Haggai and Zechariah. A first step towards the consolidation of these groups was taken with the re-establishment of the Jewish community under Ezra and Nehemiah. We must perhaps take into account here a certain ambivalence on the part of the eschatological groups. They must have been in agreement with the consolidation of a situation that was still fluid; the exceptional position of the new theocracy as expressed in law and cult must also have corresponded to their understanding of Israel. But that the constitution of a community limited to Judah and Benjamin should be widely considered to have put an end to hopes of restoration could hardly be harmonized with the prophetic promises and could hardly have been approved, therefore, by the eschatological groups. At any rate, the transmission and shaping of the hope for re-unification, for instance, show that in these circles there was a very irregular understanding of theocracy at work, which allowed for variations and changes; on their view the final step to the theocratic Israel had not yet been taken; the eschatological viewpoint, therefore, was a necessary supplement that could not be omitted. Consequently, however much these groups felt that they were members of the theocracy, they must have regarded it as their task to foster the hope of a more comprehensive restoration of Israel. This must have involved differences with the leaders of the theocracy. A further and probably more radical break took place with the events in the last decades of the fourth century B.C., with the collapse of Persian rule and the beginning of the Hellenistic expansion in the political sphere, the Samaritan schism in the cultic sphere and the interpretation of history on confessional lines by the Chronicler in the theological sphere. We think it is possible to recognize in the last chapters of the Book of Zechariah the protest of eschatological circles against the non-eschatological view of the Chronicler, who, it may be assumed, represents the official line within the theocracy. The picture of a fresh appearance of Yahweh amid the unrest and changes of the nations of the world probably communicated considerable buoyancy to the eschatological faith; but the interpretation of these events by Israel was certainly not unanimous. Over against the de-eschatologized interpretation, which regards historical disturbances as times of crisis which can be withstood with the help of Israel's institutions and religious faith,[1] is now set the eschatological interpretation of historical events, which tells of painful tribulations, before Yahweh enters upon his eschatological rule on Zion. The intensification of the eschatological aspect is only intelligible against the background of an intensification of the more or less latent differences within the Jewish community. This is the beginning of a development which ends in conflict not just between two parts of Israel, but between Israel and Israel; for on both sides there were those who considered themselves members of a theocracy; the eschatological groups also lived by the community principle which had been dominant since the formation of the Jewish community. But only one or the other view could represent 'the true Israel', while the opposing party were bound to incur the reputation of heretics. An internal Jewish split was avoided, to be sure, in the first century of the Greek era during the long period of Ptolemaic supremacy in Asia Minor and in the East Mediterranean. But the result of these conflicts, which gradually increased, and of the conventicle-type breakaways, was the gradual transformation of the restoration eschatology—which was essentially still monistic in its appearance and was regarded up to then as a faith-strengthening supplement to the theocracy, and for this purpose could use individual Parseeistic-dualistic ideas in an illustrative capacity—into the dualistic-apocalyptic form of eschatology. This, then, was the second way in which theocracy and eschatology began to be connected; the theocratic community began to regard itself as a constituent of Yahweh's heavenly kingdom, to emerge in the eschatological revolution as part of the new aeon, when the substance of this world passes away. This line, leading from Trito-Zechariah via the final stage of the Isaiah-Apocalypse to the Book of Daniel, accurately reflects, it seems to me, the development and transformation of the eschatological hope. But a complex structure like the Isaiah-Apocalypse shows very clearly that there was still room for the juxtaposition of different types of expectation. In spite of the cosmic transformation in Isa. xxiv the eschatological drama ends in the conciliatory picture of the future painted by restoration eschatology, namely the universal banquet of the nations on Zion with Israel in the centre (Isa. xxv. 6–8). The increasing severity of the conflicts, however, compelled

[1] The Jewish legend about Alexander recorded by Josephus (Ant. xi. 8. 4–5) and also the report of the attempt by Heliodorus, the Seleucid Chief Minister, to plunder the Temple at Jerusalem (2 Macc. iii. 9f.) may serve as examples of how victory over historical tribulation by representatives of the theocracy was painted in legendary colours at a later date.

the individual to assent to the eschatological faith; hence, the prospect of individual restoration was set before the believer in the form of victory over death (Isa. xxvi. 11f.). The picture of the future drawn by restoration eschatology has been interpreted, therefore, in a subsequent but consistent gloss by a reference to the abolition of death (Isa. xxv. 8aα). Finally, the Book of Daniel promises personal resurrection to those who hold fast to the eschatological faith in times of severe persecution, while those who reject this faith, although they share in the resurrection by virtue of being members of the theocracy, undergo a worse fate than the heathen world which is excluded from the hope of resurrection. It may be noted in passing —it is really outside the scope of our present study—that this assumption of personal resurrection, which was derived from the eschatological faith of the individual, was also taken up in times of testing by those who were less committed to the eschatological faith but had 'risked their lives' in an apparently hopeless struggle to live according to the commandments of their fathers.

It may perhaps be assumed that this final step in the structuring of eschatological expectations prior to the form of apocalyptic that we find in the Book of Daniel was taken during the half century in which Antiochus III came to power and the Seleucids sought to conquer Palestine and dethrone the Ptolemies, a period which involved the Jewish community in fresh disturbances and which finally brought the Seleucids success after their initial failures. The fact that the Hellenistic spirit at that time could penetrate Palestinian Judaism on a wider scale may have suited the more vigorous cultural policy of the Seleucids, whereas the Lagids, who were also of Greek origin, had been compelled to show greater restraint on the soil of the most religious nation in the ancient world and were able to continue the tolerant religious and cultural policy of the old Pharaohs. But this almost militant feature in the conduct of the Seleucids, which should not be over-emphasized, no longer encountered close resistance in the influential circles of the Jerusalem theocracy. It seems to me that long and growing neglect of the eschatological faith, sterile persistance in an outdated position and the lack which this entailed of a relevant witness gave considerable assistance to the penetration of Hellenism. Nevertheless it was quite a long time before any opposition capable of defending itself appeared. It was only the lamentable failure of the leading circles of the theocracy after the disgraceful treatment of Onias III by the Seleucid regime and the attitude of the king in the matter of the High-Priesthood that brought into the open, however hesitantly, the forces of opposition; and in their ranks the eschatological groups, for whom we may now use the description common in 1 Macc., *Hasidim*, never played the leading rôle. Yet this reserve is understandable if we remember that this group expected the great revolution to come from Yahweh in the first instance and preferred to suffer martyrdom patiently and passively rather than anticipate the coming of Yahweh by active resistance, an attitude which may have been more straightforward and honourable, but which was not particularly suited to leading an opposition. We must not imagine, therefore, that the resistance movement that was gathering beneath the Maccabean standard was a united affair, and its swift decline after only a few years attests that it was composed of very different elements. At the same time it must be remembered that 1 Macc., to which we owe the most reliable reports on the Jewish insurrection, may have been inclined to pay insufficient attention to the participation of eschatological groups of *Hasidim* because of its pro-Hasmonaean position and in view of the conflict which broke out later between groups formerly engaged in joint action.

In this present study we shall not embark on a description of the further course of the story that commences with the Maccabean revolt. Our aim has been to reconsider the period from the formation of the Jewish theocracy to the Maccabean revolt, a period which lies somewhat in the shadow of Old Testament research. For there is no doubt that it was in this period of more than two hundred years that the assumptions were formed which carried considerable weight in the further course of Jewish history and—positively or negatively—in the world of the New Testament also. The fairly peaceful pictures of the Jewish community of this period that are familiar to us depend not least on the fact that, compared with earlier and later periods of history, we possess only a few sources and even the date of these is not certain. Such a deficiency cannot be simply set aside; but it can at least be partly balanced by attempts to insert existing traditions in a wider context and to consider them from a more comprehensive point of view. This is what we have attempted here; the result is understandably of a hypothetical character and should only be regarded as a suggestion, therefore, as to how the historical connections in this obscure period might be traced more clearly. It does seem, however, from our examination that the conventional picture of the peaceful life of the Jewish community, which finally slid innocently unprepared into the religious conflict with Antiochus IV, requires revising. There was no shortage of deep-seated differences within the community and it seems quite likely to me that the tension between theocracy and eschatology was responsible for these differences; the recorded events of this period, not exactly plentiful but nevertheless significant, had a great deal to do with the intensification of these differences. This requires underlining briefly once more in our closing remarks.

Insofar as it was not possible to determine the exact significance of the eschatological hope in the exilic and early post-exilic period because of the uncertainty as to what was to become of the defeated Israel in the future, it was probably chiefly the picture of the restoration eschatology, a *restitutio in integrum*, that exercised an attractive and formative influence. Within an organized community afflicted by misfortune an eschatological faith that strives for peace and perfection can develop vital energies. But Israel's position, shattered by political catastrophe, may well be summed up in the sentence that it was not yet clear what would become of it. At such times eschatological faith may represent a permanent element of unrest, which thwarts every attempt to arrive at a new order. The consolidation which had become necessary and was attempted in the formation of the Jewish community under Ezra and Nehemiah meant, therefore, that, however much the eschatological faith was esteemed in the past, for the present eschatological expectations would undergo severe restrictions, and this is noticeable externally in territorial limitation and in the express refusal to restore the old Israel. The eschatological groups, however, for whom the collection, transmission and spiritual interpretation of the prophetic writings was important, could not declare their agreement with this exclusive position. A stabilization of the situation in the way proposed at that time may have appeared desirable to them also, because this would adequately re-affirm Israel's special position among the nations of the world; but to regard this as the complete fulfilment of the prophetic promises and to abandon the cultivation of what had become their life must have seemed intolerable to them. They felt they were members of the new community, but they did not feel obliged to surrender the eschatological expectations which were constantly imparting new strength to their faith and piety. Thus, the last century of Persian rule may have been occupied by the hidden struggle as to whether a theocracy could be based on the eschatological faith and still remain a theocracy, or whether a life *in statu promissionis* must ultimately lead to the dissolution of a theocracy. The transmission and arrangement of hopes of a restoration of the old Israel, hopes which historically belong to an earlier epoch, not only implies that surviving pieces of tradition should not be rejected, but it is also the expression of opposition to the view that the present position was definitive and final.

The political changes which led to the collapse of the Persian Empire meant along with other consequences a revival of eschatological expectations in those groups which were committed to the eschatological faith. It must have been all the more painful when the Samaritan schism, which was connected directly or indirectly with the political changes, provided effectual confirmation of the view of the exclusive theocratic circles that were opposed to them; this view was given a historical-theological rationale not long afterwards in the work of the Chronicler. It could no longer be concealed that loyalty to the eschatological faith on the soil of a theocracy that was no longer united was bound to result in a transformation of eschatological hopes, perhaps in such a way that the community within the Jewish theocracy that depended on the eschatological faith was compelled to regard itself as the true Israel; it might await the expected eschatological revolution to confirm its faith in its membership of the heavenly kingdom and consequently it could promise the individual believer the prospect of personal resurrection as a pledge. This describes the beginnings of the apocalyptic eschatology which gradually assumed more definite shape in the first century of the Greek period, while retaining several important features of the restoration eschatology, prior to attaining a comparative compactness in the decades after Antiochus III came to power and prior to the religious conflict under Antiochus IV. We may assume that there was some connection between the gradual development of a more tightly-knit apocalyptic view and an increasing separatism on the part of the eschatological groups in whose midst the apocalyptic picture of the future took shape, so that according to the testimony of I Maccabees the eschatological group of *Hasidim* possessed a fairly fixed form at the time of the religious conflict.

This hypothesis, which has been put forward in the form of a historical survey, presses to be taken further—both forwards and backwards. After long reflection this has not been done. For a continuation of the survey into the Maccabean-Hasmonaean period would have involved more use of the documents now available through the manuscript discoveries near the Dead Sea. But at the moment it seems advisable to wait until fuller studies of these texts produce a somewhat more unified interpretation. An extension of the survey backwards would have more to commend it; this was, in fact, intended and a start was made on this in the preliminary work for the present study. But it became apparent that too comprehensive a study of the eschatological literature in the prophetic writings would have been required; this would have obscured the aim of the present examination too much and consequently it will be presented separately in due course. In addition there are some problems, which I am not yet sufficiently clear about, *viz.*, among others, the affinity of the later wisdom literature, as found in some chapters of the first part of the Book of Proverbs (ch. viii and ix), for instance, to the apocalyptic view of the world. There is also the question of a renewed examination of the way in which the canon of the Old Testament was formed; according to the hypothesis presented here the collectors and interpreters of the prophetic writings, i.e. the eschatological groups, are more responsible for the formation of the prophetic canon than the leading circles of the theocracy, pre-eminently priests, to whom we owe the formation of the Pentateuch. The combination of the two parts, law and prophets, raises a series of questions which need thorough examination in view of the suggestions made above. It seems advisable, therefore, to wait until a critical assessment of the present study, in which understanding and allowance must be made for the exaggerations and onesidedness that undoubtedly occur—deliberately, in the interests of clarity, has done its necessary work.

INDEX OF PASSAGES CITED

SUBJECT INDEX

INDEX OF AUTHORS